In a world where we are bombarded by media messages to be more successful, more happy, more ambitious, more attractive; it is sometimes difficult to stand back and value our achievements. Often, especially in a crisis, we feel unable to cope and underestimate our abilities even more so.

Tom Crabtree, well known for his regular column in *Cosmopolitan* magazine, takes a realistic look at strategies for coping and meeting the challenges of everyday life. There is no instant recipe for success but with warmth, optimism and enthusiasm he persuades us that in coping confidently we are then free to make choices and implement change.

TOM CRABTREE'S
GUIDE TO

Coping

GAIN THE CONFIDENCE
TO CHANGE YOUR LIFE

UNWIN PAPERBACKS
London   Sydney

First published in Great Britain by Unwin ® Paperbacks, an imprint of Unwin Hyman Limited, in 1987

UNWIN HYMAN LIMITED
Denmark House, 37–39 Queen Elizabeth Street,
London SE1 2QB
and
40 Museum Street, London WC1A 1LU

Allen & Unwin Australia Pty Ltd
8 Napier Street, North Sydney, NSW 2060, Australia

Allen & Unwin New Zealand Ltd with the Port Nicholson Press,
60 Cambridge Terrace, Wellington, New Zealand

British Library Cataloguing in Publication Data

Crabtree, Tom
  Tom Crabtree's guide to coping : gain
  the confidence to change your life.
1. Self-confidence
I. Title
158′.1   BF575.S/
ISBN 0–04–440060–8

Set in 10 on 11 point Times Roman by Grove Graphics, Tring, and printed in Great Britain by Billing and Sons Ltd, London and Worcester

Contents

			page	
Introduction			*page*	vii
Chapter	*1*	Ideal fictions		1
Chapter	*2*	The magic helper		14
Chapter	*3*	Attitude is all		29
Chapter	*4*	The enemy within: negative feelings		43
Chapter	*5*	Worried Blue Eyes, Cheltenham		58
Chapter	*6*	More thoughts on the 'body beautiful'		70
Chapter	*7*	Friendship		84
Chapter	*8*	Sex and love		96
Chapter	*9*	Marriage		111
Chapter	*10*	The family		128
Chapter	*11*	Work and play		145
Chapter	*12*	Getting yourself together		159
Useful addresses				171

Introduction

'Isn't coping a sort of, well, *negative* word?' she asked me. I knew what she meant. Managing, getting by, keeping your head above water. 'It's hardly living,' she added. 'Living is having some choice.'

I wasn't sure what to say. I mentioned the OED definition of coping: *contend successfully with (person; task), (colloq.) deal competently with situation or problem*. I agreed that living is to have some control over your life, to be the billiard cue and not the ball. 'Some people would settle for just being able to cope,' I said, somewhat ungraciously.

When she had gone I sat down and thought about it long and hard. I thought about my own life. *When* had I started to cope − to manage, to shake off negative feelings, to start to set myself realistic goals, and achieve them. *When* had I started living, to make choices, to reach out to a few moonbeams, and be who I really was?

It had taken a long time. As a teenager I read Freud (you can imagine what a pain I was) in an attempt to understand my mother and why it was that whenever I asked her what was for tea, she would get up and go and play the piano. This was my own Riddle of the Sphinx. I never did solve it. 'Why didn't you make your own tea?' somebody asked me recently when I told her this story. Absolutely. I was big enough to stand on my own two feet, take some responsibility for myself. It wasn't until I was 34 that I looked, for the first time, at my mother as a *real* person. I stopped blaming her, wanting her to be ideal, wanting her to be the person *I* wanted her to be (and allowing her to be the person *she* wanted to be). It had been a long journey.

As a student, I had met Freud's housekeeper (in the Freuds' home in London) and she had chatted with me and shown me photographs of Freud's mother as a young woman; she had been very beautiful. All this fascinated me. Sigmund Freud had an Oedipus complex (who wouldn't, with a mother like that?), but I had an even bigger one. I attended courses at the Tavistock

Clinic and I learned to look at the world through the eyes of Sigmund Freud.

My first job was working with a man called Joshua Bierer, a Harley Street psychiatrist, and a follower of the theories of Adler. He found the first day hospital in this country and his work – with groups – was revolutionary and seminal. I learned that human beings don't have to keep looking back to the past. In a group, the patient received acceptance, affirmation and encouragement from the other members of the group. He or she was encouraged to look at the present and the future, rather than the past and to take courage to be himself/herself and to lead his/her own life.

This is old hat now, but it was completely new then. I learned, slowly, to eschew Freud, to believe that I could reach out to people who would enhance and encourage me, rather than to worry, in a purposeless, neurotic sort of way, about my mother. I started to worry about *me*: my attitudes, feelings, love life, friendships, work. I stopped wanting those others to be ideal. I began to see them as real people, not perfect, with faults, but still in with a chance of living their lives. I started to see myself in that way too. *I* stopped trying to be perfect.

I accept – now – that I'm 5′ 7″ tall, balding, but with good teeth. My body is most peculiar. My legs are my best asset (not so useful in a man, you might say, as a chorus girl but I have learned to accentuate the positive and to accept the good features of myself, as well as my faults). I've also learned to take those messages with which the media bombard us in this modern age with a very large pinch of salt.

What are those messages? For men, it is that if you buy a certain kind of deodorant or after-shave, you'll instantly become tall, handsome and rich. You won't. You'll end up confused and lost. You'll end up as I ended up in my search for the ideal mother. There are no ideal men. There's only you – the person you are, or could be.

For women the message is: stay young and beautiful if you want to be loved. Where is the hope, the truth and the affirmation of your own individuality in such a message? It's worse than Freud, who claims it all happens in childhood; we're all tethered to the gate-post of the past; our lives are pre-determined. They're *not*. Riddled with anxiety about their looks and their bodies, fretting and fussing, trying to be like that lady in the TV ad, or in the pages of that magazine, women waste their lives striving for some ideal myth. It's sad. It's a waste of time. Nobody needs to be perfect. We can all be beautiful in our own way.

No wonder so many of us can't cope. No wonder so many of us lack confidence in ourselves. I, like you, am assailed by images of the ideal figure, the ideal face, the ideal woman, the ideal kitchen. Those images are invented mostly by people who are trying to sell you shampoo, hair-conditioner, cars, clothes, kitchens or cat food. They enter the mind, though, and stay there, disturbing us, worrying us, making us feel less good about ourselves. It's like a drawingpin rattling about in a vacuum cleaner. The thing is to switch off, get rid of what's bothering us and start all over again. To have a sound self-regarding sentiment, a good self-image, we have to see that lady in the TV ad for what she is; an actress, made up, in artificial light, just playing a part. We have to learn to be real.

Freud was a *very* obsessional man. He liked things − and people − to be perfect. Alder and Bierer just wanted people to be more themselves. Being better doesn't mean being perfect. Trying to be perfect just adds to your stresses, puts one more pressure on yourself. Why set impossible goals when you can set goals that you can achieve? Why not reach out to action and happiness rather than to introspection and worry about things that don't matter?

I've learned new attitudes. I wouldn't have the nerve to lie somebody on a couch and ask them about their maternal grandmother. I lie on my own couch, start with me. What am I up to? What am I avoiding? Why do I want other people (or myself) to be perfect. Why can't I relax a bit more, accept myself a bit more, accept that people *are* often anxious and frightened? In this world, if you're not a little bit anxious you're likely to be more than a little bit potty.

There *are* people who are anxious *all the time*, scared *all the time*. They don't want to look like somebody out of *Dallas* or *Dynasty*; there are women who don't want 22″ waists; there are men who don't want to be 6′ 6″ tall and incredibly handsome. These people would be glad to be able to cope, to get through the day. For them *coping* (ie, getting through the day) has to come before living (ie reaching out to the happiness within you).

Today is a good time to start. It took me half a lifetime to start getting my values right, to sort out myself (not my mother), to get rid of all those negative feelings, impossible dreams, and

ix

that poor self-image. It took me years to realize that I didn't have to be perfect, that I was worth something and I had achieved, not perfection, but *some* success, *some* happiness, *some* courage.

My aim is to save you some time in your voyage of discovery, to stop you going down roads that lead nowhere, to save you the pain of pursuing goals that lead only to more unhappiness. What is success? It's being the best possible you. It isn't pursuing those ideal images in the media, pursuing the 'success' of wall-to-wall carpeting, a fast car (and a 22″ waist). Life is a lot more important and precious than that.

I want to try to help you to face up to coping and then to move on to living. To live *your* life, be who you were meant to be, and not anybody else, not some ideal person that others want you to be or some ideal image that you saw on TV. Television, like Plato's cave, is a world of flickering shadows. Those images are not real. The real world is found in building up networks with other people who enhance and encourage your sense of well-being and who do not fill you with a sense of failure and loss.

When you've read the book, I want you to sit down and think about your life long and hard. Where are you going? What are you achieving? Why aren't you coping − or living? What's unnecessary in your life − and why don't you get rid of it? Do you have to carry so much excess emotional baggage? I want to change your life, for the better. I want to change you, for the better. This doesn't mean that you have to be more beautiful, slimmer, better dressed. It means that you have to be you, be who you were meant to be, and have a little more faith in yourself.

Freud's central concept was insight. Go back into the past, find the complex, talk about it. Unravel the ball of wool, find the knot, untie it. The snag (excuse the pun) is that insight without resolve is useless. The patient, when he/she has been psychoanalysed, still has to find the courage to deal with the stresses and strains of everyday life. If, by reading this book, you gain some insight into yourself I shall be happy. I shall be even happier if you gain courage. Freud was concerned with what you *think* about it; Adler was concerned with what you do about it. Doing something about it takes courage. Courage is a central Adlerian concept. It is *very* important.

Don't try too hard. You'll get there; just have confidence in yourself; take small, but firm, steps. The main thing is to be heading in the right direction. In the modern world there is too much noise. From all that noise we have to pick out meaning; to receive the messages that mean something to us and to ignore those that have no real meaning whatsoever.

I wish you luck in your own journey of discovery. It's hard at times, it takes longer than you think, but it's very exciting — to have confidence in yourself, to believe in yourself, to live your own life. It's a little like old age — after all, what's the alternative? What is the point in trying to lead a life that wasn't meant for you, be somebody you were never meant to be? Better to be you than that lady with the funny shoulders in *Dallas*. Do it for you, not for her. If you're a man and you wear designer stubble, do it for you, not because you think it may bring you a turbo-charged sports car and instant success.

I can't offer any recipes for instant success. I can only show how not to undervalue your achievements and your abilities. I can encourage you to stand back and take a good look at your life, and your values. I can show you how to expect crises and how to cope with them, by not underestimating your strengths. I can show you how to accept the weaknesses within you, and, where you can, to do something about them.

Then, having worked out your strategies for *coping*, I hope you'll move on to *living*, to making choices, to being able to say, 'It's *my* life.' You'll be frightened some of the time, scared stiff some of the time, but you'll have good, fulfilling times too. Living is being who you were meant to be and nobody else. Living is being who you are, not an image, an illusion that somebody else has dreamed up for you.

Life isn't easy. In fact it can be extremely tough. I think the way to a 'better life', a 'better you', isn't to aim for some impossible dream. It's to work, with courage and hope, towards those things that you want. You can get them; it's up to you. Better to be slightly frightened and you, than somebody else and depressed and confused. After reading the book, I hope you'll make some choices of your own — that's living.

TOM CRABTREE'S
GUIDE TO
Coping

Chapter 1

Ideal fictions

If I walk out of the house and turn right I very quickly come to a main road. Quite a few times a car has drawn up alongside me on this main road and somebody, brandishing a map, has asked me, 'Can you tell me the way to Compton Acres?' (These are beautiful public gardens not far from where I live.) I can. I know the directions off by heart. I rattle them off and I can see that the occupants of the cars are impressed. Why shouldn't they be? I *know* how to get to Compton Acres.

Let's imagine, though, that the passenger or driver had stuck his/her head out of the car window and asked, 'How can I be happy?' (Or 'How can I cope with life?') That's a little bit trickier and there's no easy answer to that question.

Take coping. We've all had days when we've coped well and we've had days when we simply haven't been able to cope with anything, days when we feel that it might have been better to stay in bed and just not bother.

There are three main ways in which we can help other people to cope. We can:

Listen to them. This gives them a chance to express their feelings about a situation (or person), to talk about the problem (rather than to keep it to themselves). They may, by talking about it, see it more clearly, or even find a solution. Here, we don't come up with any answers but we may, by the way in which we listen and try to pick up the other person's feelings, indicate that we *care*. That alone can help.

For example, last week I had a call from a friend. 'Can I come round and see you?' she asked. She seemed very upset and half an hour later she was in my study sobbing her heart out. 'I've got so many things to do.' she said. 'I can cope with the job, I enjoy it, and I can cope with the kids, but the roof's leaking, there's a slate missing, and the water's coming into Mark's

1

bedroom. That's the straw that broke the camel's back. I can't cope with it. What the hell's happening to me?'

All I said to her was, 'You talk, I'll listen.' She talked for the next hour or so. Then she got up, wiped her eyes and said, 'Thanks!' Why had she thanked me? Well, I had listened – not everybody is a good listener (talking is much easier) – and I had respected her pain. She went back home. The next day she rang to say that she'd arranged for somebody to fix the roof for £20 (which she could afford) and she was feeling better. *How* listening to people makes them feel better we're not sure. The fact of the matter is that, more often than not, it does.

Give them advice. We can point out options, clarify choices, say, 'You can do A, B or C.' We can't force people to make a sensible choice, we can only help them see what choices are available to them and hope they choose the one that's most suitable for them. We can give the best advice we can to that person, in those circumstances, and hope for the best. The rest is up to the person, or to luck, or to God, depending on one's vision of the world.

Tell them something inspiring, encouraging. Hearing about other people's experiences can sometimes help us. I remember reading in the *Reader's Digest*, some years ago, about a lady who was interned in a Japanese prisoner-of-war camp. She was locked for most of the day in a tiny prison cell. What she did was to think of all the cities in the world she would like to visit, including Rome, Vienna, Berlin, Florence, Madrid and Venice, then she worked out how far it was from her prison cell to each city. Next she measured the distance across her cell. Each day she walked and walked, across the floor of her cell, there and back, from one wall to another, thousands of miles, visiting each city. At the end of the war she was freed from her prison and she really did go to all the cities she had 'visited', one by one, in her tiny cell.

In the dark days, when I find it hard to cope, I find it useful to remember that story. To me it says something about human courage, determination and the will to survive. Often, when the bad times come, we have to learn to hold on, to have courage and do our best, until the good times come again or we regain our confidence in ourselves and in our ability to resolve the problems that confront us.

Somebody once said to me that life is a series of problems to be solved. I find that a bit dreary as a definition of life. What about joy, moments of ecstasy, adventure, love, magic? Life, I hope, isn't just a series of problems (though sometimes it may seem to be). What I would agree with is that we have to make real decisions in life, we have to *choose*. Some people seem to get by without making any real decisions, by letting other people do the choosing for them, doing what other people want them to do, being what other people want them to be. Some people, perhaps, never make a real decision in their lives. I can't believe that such an attitude leads to a fulfilling and happy existence.

My own view is that, in order to be happy, we have to make real decisions, we have to be 'inner-directed' as well as 'other-directed'. It means we have to paint our own picture on the canvas of life, be who we were meant to be, achieve our potential and be able to say, 'I did it my way.'

I'm not saying it is easy. To be at ease in life you have to wear your own shoes, shoes that fit you, shoes in which you feel comfortable. Many of us are tempted to wear shoes that are expensive and which make the right impression, but they're not our shoes; they were meant for other people, not us, and that's why we feel ill-at-ease.

The shoes we wear have different names: pretence, imitation, fear, unhappiness, stress, false goals, ideal fictions, 'success'. We were meant to grow, like trees and shrubs, into the full flowering of our being; instead of that many of us grow in a fragmented, *ad hoc* way, trailing behind us cynicism and/or despair. Why does it happen? Human beings were *not* meant to be happy all the time, that's simply impossible. They weren't meant to be miserable all of the time either. Why do we spend so much of our lives feeling alienated, ill-at-ease with ourselves and/or others, feeling that we have little control over our own existence?

Last year I met a mother who told me that she had a 4-year-old son with a very loud voice. 'Exactly how loud is it?' I asked her. 'Deafening,' she answered, 'like the foghorn of an ocean-going liner.' It really did get on her nerves. What I did was to show the boy how the volume of a radio is controlled, by a knob turned to the right or left. Then, we tied a coffee-jar lid to a circle of string and hung it around his neck so that the 'volume knob' rested on his chest. 'Down a bit,' his mother would say when his voice boomed out. The boy soon learnt to control the volume of his own voice and remind himself to speak more

3

quietly. *He took responsibility for his own voice* and brought an aspect of his response-ability to others under his own control. Other children liked him more. At the age of 4 he'd started to learn an important principle of life: *we can take over the reins of our own behaviour and of our own lives if we go about it the right way.*

Yet how many of us adults do manage this? Many of us live our lives as though we were billiard balls with somebody else always holding the cue, knocking us this way or that, putting us into this pocket or that, deciding when the game should finish or start. We are the game. We are our own voice. We should sing and dance to our own tune rather than be jerked about like puppets on a string or dance like bears to somebody else's insistent, strident melody. We must learn to be who we are. So how do we do it?

To get to the starting line for living we have to learn to accept ourselves and this means being a little kinder to ourselves. I know people who are very hard on themselves indeed. It is as though life is a competition and they have to beat everybody in sight; or as if, when they have achieved something, they can't accept it as an achievement. Such people have a very poor sense of their own worth; they feel unable to say, 'I belong to this earth and I have as much right to walk on this planet as anybody else. I do belong here, so I'm going to be good to myself and hold my head up high.' The real competition in life is with yourself: to strive to be the person you were meant to be to the full.

Most of us punish ourselves relentlessly: we'd like to be taller/slimmer/more attractive; we'd like to have blue/brown eyes or a 22″ waist. The energy spent on worrying about the things we can't change *could* be spent on changing the things we can change: things that would enhance our lives and make us much happier human beings.

Take ideal fictions. In all our heads, in the theatre of our unconscious mind, there strolls about the ideal mother, the ideal father, the ideal family, the ideal figure, the ideal woman, the ideal man. Do they exist anywhere else, these ideal people? Yes. They exist on television. There we see ideal mothers cleaning the kitchen floor or washing the dishes and looking as though they've just come out of a beauty salon. It may be fiction but it is dispiriting. It makes you feel, if you are a mother, (a) guilty and (b) inadequate. Why aren't your kitchen floors like that? Why do you always look, when you've been looking after the

4

children, as though there's been a train accident and you've just scrambled down the embankment? You look like that because you are human, like the rest of us. The ideal mother doesn't exist. But this, somehow, isn't enough, you still worry about your hair, your figure (and that hell-hole you laughingly call a kitchen).

It happens to men too. In my mind's eye I am tall, with blue eyes and have an unyielding stare. Women are crazy about me. It's not my mind they're after: it's my body. The slim, taut frame and my long legs (not to mention my craggy, clean-shaven face with the high cheek bones) seem to hold an irresistible fascination for women everywhere. It is with difficulty that they refrain from hurling themselves upon me when I walk through Woolworths or any large department store.

The reality is somewhat different. I am 5' 7" tall, with brown/hazel eyes and my figure is strikingly reminiscent of a large beach ball. When I go to the tailor and look in the mirror I see Oliver Hardy looking back at me in the mirror, moustache, baldness and all. There was a time I used to worry about this dreadfully. Now, I really do believe it doesn't really matter all that much. Most of my friends are so obsessed with their own worries about their hair/faces/figures that they don't really notice. When we worry about that sort of thing, we worry alone.

Some things are perfect, but not people. When I look at a painting by Rembrandt, or a sculpture by Michelangelo, to my eye they're quite lovely, perfect. So are Mozart's music, one or two poems by Philip Larkin, and one or two short stories by J. D. Salinger. I can understand the search for artistic perfection. What I am against is striving for perfection in our looks, our figures, our friendships, love affairs, marriages and families. They're all spoken about in an ideal, mythical way. It does the confidence of each and every one of us no service at all.

Take looks. Do your ears inspire laughter, your mouth defy the camera? Join the club. It's only film stars and those models on TV who have the kind of looks you dream about. The rest of us have faces that look lived in *and* we're the great majority. You're not beautiful and neither am I. Who needs it?

I'll modify that. You may well be beautiful in the eyes of somebody — and that's what counts. Beauty, as far as people are concerned, *is* in the eye of the beholder. There is no ideal against which we can all be measured. Ideas about facial beauty change from age to age and from country to country. My

5

mother had a round face and a peaches-and-cream complexion, with a small rose-bud mouth. In her day, she was considered beautiful. Now, more angular, less rounded faces are the vogue.

I once met a woman in a laundrette who asked me, 'Do you keep losing socks?' I held up one leg to reveal a trim, but sockless, ankle. We started chatting about this and that and I asked her to have coffee with me. Over coffee we discussed sexual attractiveness and I told her that she scored 8 out of 10 on the Sexual Attractiveness Scale (well, she *did* have a very full figure and her hair looked like a sawn-off toothbrush). I never saw her again. Only a psychologist could be so stupid. What women wants to be told facts, the truth? What she wants to know is that you *see* her as beautiful. She knows perfectly well that you could be biased.

Have you ever thought what it would be like to be beautiful? (I'll be saying more about this later.) Being beautiful is like being royal, it cuts you off from spontaneous reaction, from friendship and from fun. Beauty is power. If you're beautiful, people overrate your abilities, men are scared of you. You'd never be sure whether men liked you for yourself or purely for your looks. You'd be terrified of growing old and losing those looks. Where's the fun in being beautiful?

I once read about a film star who was never asked out for a date. Men just assumed that anybody so beautiful would have no time for *them*. Meanwhile, the film star's secretary was always being asked out, men found her more approachable, more in their league, less frightening. Being beautiful can be very lonely. Nobody, if you're beautiful, says, 'What are you doing next Tuesday?' They just wouldn't dare.

Beauty may arouse admiration and adulation; it can also cause loneliness and isolation. What we should be doing is not chasing the myth of perfect beauty, but enjoying *ourselves*, making the best of *ourselves* (and finding a partner who appreciates our qualities and, hopefully, thinks we're beautiful even when we're not).

It's the same with the 'body beautiful'. Nearly every woman I know is constantly worried about her weight. (It's those models on TV again. Models need to be thin: it makes the clothes look better on film and in magazines, especially when the clothes are pinned up at the back as they often are in those glossy photos.) Many women say to me, 'I wish I could lose 6 lb.' This wouldn't be significant, except that most of these women are, in my view, positively skinny. I tell them that a man needs something to get hold of but it doesn't seem to provide any reassurance.

Most of us, body-wise, don't look as though we have stepped out of a television advertisement or from the page of a glossy magazine. Some of us are shaped like pencils, some like bean-bags, some like beach balls. In my time I've fallen in love with women of most peculiar shapes. What attracted me was some 'X' factor, some sexy quality that they exuded. I know a very jolly lady of 13 stone who has plenty of men friends. I think it's partly because she gives out, enjoys herself, doesn't spend most of her life worrying about her figure.

I have no objection to any human being wanting to avoid obesity, wanting to be fit, to feel good; that's common sense. The pursuit of the ideal figure isn't. I don't say that because, personally, I am not attracted by women who resemble fishing rods. I say it because I object to other people imposing mythical standards of beauty on us and because women (and men) who pursue these fictitious goals are prevented from relaxing and from making warm, close relationships. How can you do that if you don't accept yourself as a viable, authentic human being, even if you do bulge slightly in the wrong places?

Later on I'll be saying more about the 'ideal figure' and the 'body beautiful' and the mental distress that such notions cause people. This includes those women who suffer from anorexia and bulimia nervosa. It includes ordinary people like you and me. It also includes beautiful people, people who have reached the ideal, created a myth; surprisingly, they don't feel any more confident than the rest of us.

In *Face Value — the Politics of Beauty* (Routledge & Kegan Paul) Robin Tolmach Lakoff and Raquel L. Scherr asked beautiful people how they felt about themselves. What they received as answers were moans of distress; 'Well, OK, but . . .' said the beautiful people and those buts covered every part of the body. It is truly amazing how lacking in confidence many beautiful people are. A wanted to be blonde, B to have curly eyelashes, C to have larger breasts, D longer legs; they all wanted to lose weight — anything from 2 to 10 kilograms. Why can't women by happy with themselves as they are? Why all this disgust when they look in the mirror? It's because they don't aim for the Best Me (which is reasonable), but for Ms Perfection (which isn't). The myth of perfection weaves its malignant spell yet again.

7

Take the myth of the perfect partner. To demand the ideal man or the ideal woman is rather like going into a restaurant and saying, 'I'll have the whole menu.' It simply will not work. What you have to do in a restaurant and what you have to do when you're choosing a partner are exactly the same: you make a choice about what you need and want. You can't have it all. I advise women (and men) to settle for a 70 per cent solution. There is always going to be something about him/her that irritates, annoys or puzzles you, because nobody is perfect. What a strain it would put on us if they were.

What makes it more difficult is that human beings often have conflicting needs, and at the same time. A woman may want − and need − a man who is dependable *and* exciting, mysterious *and* down-to-earth, moody *and* fun to be with, practical *and* deeply romantic. Do you marry a man like the one in *Room with a View* who climbs the tree and shouts, 'Love, adventure, freedom'? Or do you choose a man who can grout your bathroom? Do you go for a man who can put up shelves or opt for one who will embrace you passionately, gardening gloves and all, behind the rhododendrons? I can't tell you. You have to do the choosing. I can only tell you that the ideal man doesn't exist.

I do believe, strongly, in injecting romance into this sometimes grey and dreary world. A man I know flew over from Canada to take a woman he had met on holiday a bunch of flowers. He arrived on her doorstep, in Cornwall, in a rainstorm. He knocked on the door and, when she answered, said, 'Brought you some roses.' Rain was dripping down his face, water fell from his ears, nose and chin on to her doorstep. She asked him in. He had a bath, borrowed her bathrobe and, standing there like a new penny in her white wrap, proposed to her (*and* on his knees). Who could resist? She couldn't. I went to the wedding. It *was* romantic.

I do believe in romance. I don't believe in a feverish search for the ideal man, some 'magic helper' (more on this later). This may be the stuff of great novels, but living out the passion and excitement of great novels can be very wearing. It may also entail a complete renunciation of self, a very dangerous business. In my view, some of the men with whom women fall madly in love simply aren't up to the part. To give up one's self to a man whose real love is train sets seems to me a somewhat foolish act.

Take Madame Bovary. She was a woman of spirit and she believed in passion, ideal love. Fed up with the good doctor, she gives herself to Rodolphe. Fed up with Rodolphe, she tries Leon. With Leon, she's inflamed, tears off her corset, throws herself on his breast with a shudder, orders him not to go out, to think only of them, to love her. That kind of thing frightens a lot of men. 'I'm mad. Kiss me' – a simple enough direction. Many men, at this point, go off to the pub to talk about football with their mates. This is why I talk about the 70 per cent solution: to insist on a higher percentage in a partnership may lead to depression rather than fortune.

Are there any ideal women? I once met a man in a pub who told me that his wife didn't put his slippers out in the evening when he came home from work. 'My mother used to do that for my father,' he said. I didn't point out that his wife wasn't his mother. I didn't point out that every Persian carpet has a tiny, deliberate mistake in the design since only Allah is perfect. I think he had married a mother-figure who, in his view, had forgotten her part in the play he had devised, written and produced.

That woman wasn't unusual. Some women are expected to be housewife, good mother and seductress (or whore) in turn. 'Which fantasy figure am I playing tonight?' a woman might well ask as her husband/partner comes in through the door. Such demands are very tiring and it is hard to judge what is expected at any given moment.

A friend of mine went to an underwear party and bought a peep-through bra, some silk French knickers and black silk stockings and suspenders. 'That should do the trick,' she said to herself, two days later, as she donned her sexy apparel. She went downstairs (it was about 9.30 pm) and flung open the living-room door. Her husband was watching TV. He looked up at her in all her glory, standing there, arms akimbo. 'Are you going out?' he asked, returning to watching the weather forecast. That evening, I suspect, she was expected to be the housewife, not the vamp.

It is not easy to treat those with whom we have a loving and dependent relationship as real people, with needs and wants (and an existence) of their own. Consider the family. We all carry around in our heads the idea of the perfect family: father, mother and child(ren) living in total harmony, with never a quarrel, never a cross word. We all pay homage to the image of the good mother, gentle and kind, and the loving father. Both are lead players in the theatre of the collective unconscious.

The Madonna Complex works powerfully within us to deny that a mother could feel tired out, fed up, angry, frustrated, at screaming pitch, bewildered, lost. Our notion of a heavenly, ideal father denies that fathers get fed up and tired too, that they find the stresses and strains of family life quite considerable (even though primary child care usually falls on the mother).

Somewhere (over the rainbow?) there may be an ideal family, but I've never come across it. What I have met are families where I wonder, in the first place, why we married her (or vice versa), why they're so obsessed with tidiness, why they shout at each other all the time, why they fuss about things that don't really matter. Then, I learned that each family is different; each has its own style; each has its own way of doing things.

Every family encounters problems sooner or later. One-third of partners will divorce. Two-thirds — if the present statistics are anything to go by — will not. It doesn't mean that those partners who do not divorce have not thought of packing it in, walking out, giving up, looking for something different. They've thought about it, believe me. It's love, or commitment (or nowhere to go) that has kept them together. A family isn't meant to provide bliss, it's meant to provide a safe base from which we can make our excursions into the world. A family wasn't meant to provide for all our needs. The family is one segment in what should be a wider support system of family, relations and, especially, friends.

I used to work with a colleague who would always write on the case notes, 'Anxious mother'. One day I said to her, 'All mothers are anxious; it's being mothers that makes them like that.' Equally, fathers get tetchy, have their funny ways. If a family works in its own way, that's fine by me. I realize, now, that when I thought a family was odd all I was saying was that it wasn't like my own. But why should it be? If people quarrel, argue, shout at each other, have spells of resentment and are very much less than gruntled, then that is the norm for family life. Mary never shouted at Joseph, I know, even though Joseph wasn't very good at hotel bookings. Some wives complain when the family ends up in a hotel without *en suite* bathrooms, never mind in a stable.

Most families go through a hard time at some stage or other. Some have to face it when the children are young, some when the children are older. Tragic things happen to some families, and parents aren't to blame: bad things can happen to good people. It's a mistake to look for perfection — or bliss — within families. There will be moments of happiness, and some of sadness, good times, bad times. Bringing up children is a very hard job. Rearing a happy family is on a par with painting the Mona Lisa. It's a great achievement and it takes a lot longer.

What does the damage to mothers (and fathers) is the misguided notion that, somewhere, there is an ideal family where nothing goes wrong, where children don't have sicknesses or problems, aren't difficult, uncooperative and rebellious when they're teenagers. If you believe in the ideal family it induces a sense of failure, making you feel guilty for not being the ideal mother (or ideal father). Just remember, nobody is. A family is hard work, plus commitment, liberally sprinkled with hope and love.

In life you must learn not to pretend, but to be who you are. There is no need to imitate anybody else. We all have a place on this planet, we are entitled to be here. We will meet hard times, but we *deserve* good times too. We must learn to respect ourselves, to accept ourselves more, as we are, and to cast aside those ideal fictions which are no more than the figments of some advertising person's imagination.

So, here are ten steps towards coping with life. They will not provide an instant solution or total happiness, but they may set you off in the right direction. The key to success is your attitude. To help you gain the right attitude, to gain self-respect, you should remember the following points:

1 *Consign ideal fictions to the rubbish bin.* Ask yourself, 'Does this work for me?' If it does, that's fine. If it doesn't, do something about it. Life is too precious to waste worrying about the impression you are making on others. Remember that all relationships, if they are to succeed, have to be worked at. If you wait for the handsome prince (or the ideal woman), you will wait a very long time.

2 *Don't fear failure.* We learn more from our failures than we do from our successes. Think of yourself as an orchestra tuning up, there'll be some false notes but, with practice, one day you'll play that symphony which is you.

3 *Don't envy pop stars, famous people.* Some of them are happy, some are not. The ones that are, remain true to themselves. It's no good being able to dine at the Ritz if

your soul has disappeared in the process of becoming 'successful'. Success is feeling at one with yourself, a peace of mind. Success is to be found in all walks of life, not just among the famous.

4   *Be selective, have a style to suit you.* If somebody offers you something that isn't your style say no (a very useful word; practise saying it in the mirror). Don't model yourself on someone you have seen on TV or in a magazine. That's not you; you're a whole lot better than that.

5   *Avoid 'Yes, but . . .'* If somebody says to you, 'I think you have a marvellous figure' don't say 'Yes, but if I could lose 8 lb I'd . . .' It's nonsense. To be constantly over-critical of yourself is the psychological equivalent of jumping into a bed of nettles. Learn to say, 'I'm fine as I am.' (Or, at least, 'I'm working on me.')

6   *Don't be so hard on yourself.* You deserve to be happy from time to time, you deserve to enjoy yourself now and then. Happiness is a habit. To rediscover it, try to find friends who know what it's about and can teach you. Don't make out that life is hell all the time, it is very off-putting. Life is what you allow to happen to you, what you allow other people to do to you and life is what slips by while you are thinking about perfection.

7   *Be fit and as well-turned out as you can.* Don't get obsessed with your low-flying ears or the fact that you have only seven perfect finger nails. Concentrate on making the best of what you have. Remember that beautiful people, too, wonder whether their legs are too fat, their breasts too small, their hips too big and so on. It's human to wonder. It's foolish to let it spoil your life.

8   *Beauty is more than fashion.* It's a mixture of body *and* mind. It also has a subjective element. It's because we're so obsessed with rating scales (and those ideal fictions) that we get so depressed about it. Say out loud, 'I'm beautiful', and mean it. Who can prove you wrong?

9   *Believe yourself to be beautiful and you will be.* The secret is to smile at people. Just try it and see if it works.

10   *Be you.* It's such a strain trying to be somebody else all the time. The fact that you are not perfect is a great relief to the rest of us.

Having dealt with the ideal fictions, let's look at some strategies for coping, to discover what is effective and what isn't. Let's look at what other people can do for us — and what we can do for ourselves — to enhance the quality of our lives. Let's take a peep at that curious figure who strolls across the boards in the theatre of our minds. I've seen him in lots of productions and a very powerful performance he gives. He's called the 'magic helper' and his presence on stage certainly affects the rest of the company.

Chapter 2
The magic helper

I gave a lecture recently. Before I entered the hall where I was about to speak a lady came up to me and asked, 'Are you nervous?' I told her I was, just a little bit anxious. Why not? Anxiety is the price we pay for trying to do something difficult – the more daring the venture, the higher the anxiety. You cannot achieve in life without *some* anxiety; if you weren't anxious about certain things you wouldn't be normal.

Giving a lecture doesn't frighten me too much, but I still get anxious. A good lecture, like good writing, has to have form and soul. It has to have a shape to it, a logical sequence, a pattern. Within that shape it has to be infused with tone, wit, style, elegance, anecdote, humour. Too much style without content makes it empty, meaningless. Too much content without style and a sense of humour makes the whole thing dreary, less than entertaining.

It is exactly the same with life but, before I go on to talk about that, let me say that there *are* plenty of things that still frighten the life out of me. I couldn't be a spiderman (one of those men who walk on girders hundreds of feet above the ground) to save my life. I'm simply scared stiff of heights. On a high ladder my anxiety level reaches unmanageable limits and I have to come down. That kind of things doesn't give me the charge, the adrenalin boost, I need to get things done; it merely scares me so much that I become paralysed with fear (and slowly make my way down the ladder trembling with fright).

The way I cope with this is to avoid ladders and heights. The price, in anxiety, is too high. I could, I suppose, learn to conquer my fears by practising on small ladders, working (literally step-by-step) to conquer my fear, to reach greater heights. I don't bother. I console myself that I don't *have* to do it and that the spiderman would probably be terrified if he had to give a lecture (whereas I can do that with just enough adrenalin to pump a bit of life into my talk).

14

The optimal level of anxiety that is needed to do anything important well will vary from person to person and from task to task. One woman will think nothing of asking six people to dinner, while another will be consumed with anxiety for days beforehand. Will it go well? How will she cope? That depends on whether she lets the anxiety spur her into action or whether she lets it consume her, or reduce her usual performance level. She may be overcome with fear and ring up her guests to say, 'The dinner party's off.' She may go ahead but feel that the evening was a flop because she was so nervous. She may gather all her resources and put on a really marvellous dinner party. *What counts in life is not so much the event but how we set about tackling the event. What is important is not what happens to us but our reaction to it.*

To cope with life you need to: (a) know yourself; (b) learn to be a little bit kinder to yourself; (c) slowly build up your confidence so that you can learn to tackle things you once considered very difficult or even impossible. My sister, a few years ago, drove from Southend to Oxford with her children. No big deal, you may say, but for her it was. She had never driven such a long distance before. She felt terribly proud of herself when she'd done it. It was an achievement, it added to her confidence and she had shown courage in the face of the inevitable anxiety. It was another step in the direction of self-respect, being able to say, 'I can do it.' It takes courage and *courage* is a recurrent theme in this book.

One of the reasons that many people find it difficult to cope with day-to-day living is that they have an erroneous notion of normality. You, for example, may suspect that you are slightly peculiar, rather odd, different from the kind of people you live with, work with. You may divide humanity into a bimodal distribution, like the humps on a camel's back, with Group A (normal) over there and Group B (slightly odd, maladjusted, or frankly mad) somewhere else. If you think about it carefully you may, with some despondency, place yourself in Group B.

It doesn't help you a great deal more if you place yourself in Group A. You may strain too hard to be 'normal', spend a lot of time and energy keeping up a front, convinced that nobody but you has panic attacks or has awful days — or weeks — when they feel they simply can't cope. Worse, you will wonder about your own 'normality' and be absolutely convinced, from time to time, that you're going slightly mad, or, at the very least, turning into an eccentric.

What you need to remember is that the range of human behaviour is very wide indeed. Adjustment is a continuum and, given sufficient stress, anybody can find themselves at the wrong end of the line. My own adjustment varies throughout the week. On Monday morning I'm, frankly, maladjusted — out of tune with myself, and life. I've staged a recovery by the afternoon. By Wednesday I'm in my stride and, come the weekend, I've moved along to the 'well-adjusted' end of the continuum. I don't claim to be 'normal' at weekends, merely that I can cope better with weekends than with the stresses and strains of the working week.

Let me amend what I've said; I think I *am* normal. Normality is not being always on top. Normality is being able to cope — with life, with love, with work, with friendship. On some days I'll cope better than others; on some days I'll feel anxious; on some days I'll panic (and on one or two days I'll feel I'm really doing well). *That's* normality. Normality is not being happy all day, every day, but being able to cope (and seizing your chances of happiness when they come). If you think that normality is constant happiness then you condemn yourself to a pervasive feeling of failure (and of being 'abnormal').

With stress (and nobody I know lives without *some* stress), what counts is its (a) intensity and (b) duration. Equally important, is how you react to it. Stress always has a subjective component. The way in which you deal with stress is part of your *life-style*. A life has — like a good book — both content and style. In life, the content is what happens to people, the style is how they deal with it. Somewhere along the road of life *everybody* will show signs, whether transitory or prolonged, of not being able to cope with the stresses and strains imposed on them. Only a person with pointed ears, someone from Venus, copes with personal problems and stress with complete equanimity.

The three ways of dealing with perceived danger or stress are: (a) *fight*; (b) *flight*; (c) *imitation*. If a tiger enters your living room (and you perceive that as a dangerous situation), you can get a chair and stand your ground, make for the nearest window or pretend to be a tiger. (The last strategy I would consider to be fairly risk-laden.) In your personal life you have exactly the same three modes of defence against feelings of loss, pain, isolation, defeat, guilt, insult and sorrow. You can fight back against a world that has hurt you; you can 'run away' by withdrawing

16

into yourself (and withdrawing from other people), or you can pretend to be someone else, 'put up a front', so that nobody knows you have been hurt.

I would like to be able to say that, of these three modes of dealing with pain and stress, the best is fight. I believe it to be true but sometimes people aren't able to fight. If you have been hurt a great deal, placed under tremendous stress, you may be paralysed, almost destroyed. The emotional hurt (and emotional pain hurts just as much as being kicked on the shin, and it lasts a great deal longer) may be quite staggering. I can understand *why* you may want to pretend that you haven't been hurt as much as you have. I can understand why you may want to withdraw, nurse your pain. Some people nurse their pain for days, weeks. Some people may harbour their emotional pain for life. The pain is there. It's always with them. It's of no use to anybody to deny it exists.

The way back to life is to learn to look at the pain, hold it up to the light where you can see it clearly and to *forgive* those who are responsible. Say, 'What was, was. What is, is. I am not going to let what happened in the past make me forget that today is a new day and that I am entitled to live my life, be the best possible person I can be.' To say something like that, and act upon it, takes an enormous amount of courage. To move to living today, in the Here and Now, is a very big step indeed. Consider these two examples.

Case 1. Barbara, aged 30. Barbara is married with two young children. When she was a child she was beaten by her mother regularly, compared unfavourably with a younger sister and never shown any affection. Her childhood was a living hell. Barbara told me that, one night, her mother came upstairs, told her to get out of bed, then beat her for stealing some biscuits out of a tin. Barbara's body was covered with bruises. The next morning, at breakfast, her younger sister said that she'd eaten the biscuits. 'That's all right, darling,' her mother said. The mother didn't even apologize to Barbara for the mistake. The beatings ceased when Barbara became a teenager. The rejection, and injustice, didn't. Mother loved — and still loves — the younger sister. Even now, she has never once in her life told Barbara that she loves her.

Case 2. John, aged 35, unmarried. John's father was a loud-voiced, violent man. He could be charming and loving but, under the influence of drink, would beat up his wife — and John, if he attempted to intervene. 'He would sit me on his knee and tell me stories when I was a little boy,' John told me. 'I used to like that a lot.' When John was older he was favoured by the father and encouraged in his school work and in his attempts to become an architect. At the same time, when he'd been drinking, the father would turn physically violent and attack John's mother.

'I was just finishing my university course,' John told me, 'when I heard that my father was dying of cancer. I had not realized he was so ill. I went home to see him. I wanted to tell him that I loved him — despite the bad things — and that I appreciated all the good things he'd given me, but before I had a chance to tell him the hospital rang to say he'd died in the night. I didn't get a chance to say what I wanted to say. The next time I saw him was in a coffin. I looked at him, went outside and cried like a baby. I wanted to put things right, you see, wanted to make things straight between us. Can you understand that?'

I can. Many people have a sadness, or a resentment, or despair, that springs from unfinished business. There are things they needed to say, feelings they needed (and still need) to express, deal with, accept, talk about, gain some control over, live with. These feelings are real (emotions are *very* real) and they can have powerful effects on human behaviour.

Many people carry around with them the memory of *past* defeats and pain. They carry with them *guilt* (was I to blame?), regrets (it could have been better), bitterness, hate, jealousy, failure, anger, envy, blame and many other emotions. Dealing with feelings isn't the same as dealing with measles, or a broken arm, or a hernia. Cure is rarely a term applied to mental problems. If somebody is mentally ill, hospitalized, treated and then assessed for discharge the question is: 'Can he/she *cope* with the world outside?' The patient may be better (ie better able to function). The patient has not crossed a line on one side of which are those who are ill and those who are 'cured'. There may be a slow moving forward towards good adjustment, robust mental health — and happiness.

To see your family doctor you usually have to produce a definite symptom. This allows your dis-ease to be labelled, a treatment is suggested and you come away with the notion that there is, indeed, something specific wrong with you. You have the badge of illness conferred upon you or your symptoms are given a name. That's why many people *feel* better when they have seen the doctor about a physical symptom. At least, then, they can put a name to what is wrong and, hopefully, they will be given a course of treatment to put it right.

In the world of the emotions things are not so quick, methodical, definite (or predictable). Take Barbara's case. In my view, for Barbara to live her life to the full − ie, to start living her life in the present instead of the past, what I call getting to the starting line − she must do a number of things. What is at stake here is the *quality* of her life. She is physically well, she can cope. To be happy she would have to deal with some of the unfinished emotional business in her life. As I stressed before, this takes a great deal of courage.

One course for Barbara would be to remember the pain and to blame her mother. This would make Barbara feel some guilt (*was* she in some way responsible?) and would fill her with resentment of, and hatred for, a mother who clearly was unjust in her dealings with her and who loved her less than she deserved. Resentment and hate take up emotional energy. They also affect inter-personal relationships; it is hard to love others when one is consumed with resentment and hate.

An alternative course for Barbara would be to remember how well she had done in her life, despite her awful childhood, and look at her own family and friends. Taking strength from her achievements, she could forgive her mother. She will not forget what her mother did to her (all human beings have memories), but she can decide to see her mother as a real person, warts and all, and have the courage to say, 'I loved you as a child.' (She could add, 'I love you now' if that were the case.) This act of forgiveness clears the lumber from the attic of Barbara's mind, it takes the resentment away (and that resentment is like carrying a ton of coal on your back) and it brings Barbara to *now*.

It is not necessary for Barbara to like her mother. It is necessary for her to forgive her if she wishes to deal with the painful experiences of the past and get through the agenda of unfinished business. The first course of action − blame and resentment − means that the business is never finished. The pain lives on through Barbara, and could be passed to the next generation.

With John, there is a similar need to forgive. John told me, 'I think about by father for ten minutes every day, when I wake up, and when I've thought about him and the good and bad things he did I say out aloud, "I loved you." Then I get out of bed and live my life. That ten minutes each day is a kind of offering to him, ten minutes of memory, regrets and love. I'd rather do that than let the memory of him affect the whole of my life.' John loved his father deeply, despite the way he hurt him. He recognizes that fact, holds it up to the light and, in doing so, disentangles himself from the emotional coils of the past and gives himself permission to live.

In theory, it's easy to move from the past and all those defeats, all that pain, up to the starting line (which is today). The practice is a lot more difficult. A great many false notions and misguided goals, not to mention many people's propensity to be hard on themselves, prevent the race for happiness ever getting under way. Perhaps we should follow the advice of Alcoholics Anonymous and take life one day at a time. Try starting each day with a clean emotional sheet, try looking the Monsters − all those destructive, wasteful emotions − straight in the eye and get on with your life.

I once met a man who had a very positive philosophy of life. His guiding principle was simple: to concentrate on today and to snatch a moment of happiness from each day. 'I remember what Iago says of Othello,' he told me. ' "He hath a daily beauty in his life." I've taken those words and applied them to my own existence. Every day I say them and, whatever the circumstances, I try to look at something beautiful or do something which refreshes my soul. I walk in the rain, look up at the night sky, look at a tree, listen to a bird singing. I remember there is magic in the world, and in me.' There are those who, in adversity, reach out to life, look to the light at the end of the tunnel. There *is* light. To see it, those who are under stress must lift up their heads, they must have courage.

I've said it isn't easy to get to the starting line, to start living your life as it was meant to be lived. I mean it. There are a thousand ways in which you and I can avoid solving our problems, go about the day trailing clouds of anxiety (or followed by the big black cloud of guilt). But what do you get by way of a reward from ineffective psychological strategies? The answer is, confirmation: that you are a worthless person ('I deserve nothing better') and the unhappiness you perceive within yourself confirms your own diagnosis.

Years ago, *c.* 535 BC, there was a man who lived on the Greek island of Samos. His name was Polycrates and he built a fleet of galleys of one hundred and fifty oars, each with a huge sail and carrying, together, over a thousand Samian bowmen. With his fleet he conquered all the neighbouring islands and half of Greece. At the height of his power his friend, King Amasis of Greece, warned him that the gods did not like human beings who were too successful.

Polycrates asked Amasis what he should do to placate the gods. 'Take something precious and throw it away, as an offering to the gods,' said Amasis. Polycrates threw his favourite ring, an emerald, into the sea. Five or six days later the ring turned up in a fish that a fisherman had caught and had presented to Polycrates. When Amasis heard about the incident he ended his friendship with Polycrates, saying it was impossible for one man to save another from his destiny (and it was quite clear that the gods had it in for the Tyrant of Samos). The prophecy took root in the heart of Polycrates, he was lured to Iona by his enemies, and crucified. The prophecy became self-fulfilling.

This story means a lot to me. I have visited Samos, strolled around the harbour at Pythagoreion (the one from which Polycrates sailed out to throw away the emerald ring). I have sat in a café on one wall of which was a painting of one of the Tyrant's galleys. Samos is a very beautiful place (Anthony and Cleopatra went there for their honeymoon). It's not a place, given its tiny white houses, lemon groves, cedar and oak trees, and its famous wine, that one would associate with guilt, worry and self-punishment.

It was J. C. Flugel, in his book *Man, Morals and Society* (Penguin Books), who first coined the term the Polycrates Complex. It is used to describe those who bring disaster – financial, emotional, personal, social, vocational – on their own heads. It seems hard to believe that people would bring pain and sorrow into their own lives when there is so much hurt and anguish in the world already. However, over the years, looking at the lives of friends and acquaintances, I can see that this is the case. There are people who constantly put themselves on trial, who act as accused, judge and jury, who unremittingly pronounce a verdict of 'guilty' upon themselves.

Why do people think of themselves as 'guilty'? What terrible things have they done to bring in this self-imposed verdict? Often, they have done nothing, or very little. They were *not* the

21

cause of what went wrong in the past (other people were there too). They have not murdered, abused, cheated or stolen from another human being. Where they have done wrong, the wrongs they have done have been trivial, considering the stituation. Or the wrongs have been cries for help. Why, then, the feeling that they have committed some awful crime against the gods and deserve to be punished? What makes them *feel* so guilty? This is how it works:

The pain The pain *was* palpable, real. Some, or much, of it remains. The pain is faced up to, or added to.

The blame Something awful happens: the death of a parent, the divorce of a parent, a child being emotionally or physically abused. The child says, in effect, 'I'm to blame.' The child *isn't* to blame but the unconscious mind knows no logic.

As a grown-up the child within the adult (residing within the unconscious mind and within the realm of feeling) still points an accusing finger. The blame, despite the lack of logic, is accepted.

The guilt With the acceptance of blame comes the guilt. It is left-over childhood guilt, but it operates powerfully within adult lives. An inner voice says, 'You should be ashamed of yourself' or 'Mummy won't love you if you do that/are like that' or 'This terrible, awful thing has happened and you are guilty.' The inner voice may say, 'You are bad. Look at the bad things that have happened in your life.' (The voice never says that nobody's perfect, nobody's ideal or that bad things happen to good people.) Feeling guilty about the past solves nothing. It absolves people from dealing with the present. Who can concentrate on the present in the middle of a dramatic court case (in which one person takes all the parts)?

The shame All of us must give ourselves permission to live, permission to move up to the starting line. Laden with guilt, that permission is withheld. You and I see ourselves as worthless people who don't deserve happiness. If it comes our way we quickly provoke a situation which will destroy the happiness and confirm our own estimation of ourselves.

The strategy The strategy is, in effect, a self-fulfilling prophecy. Feeling worthless and ashamed,what are you to do? You will choose to mix with people – especially members of the opposite sex – who will hurt you. If they *don't* hurt you, you'll drop them and find somebody who does. Thus, your own estimation of yourself and your worst fears are confirmed. Fun (ie, guiltless pleasure) is something you don't reach out to, just as you don't reach out to love, ecstasy, adventure, personal fulfilment. Why? You feel you don't deserve it. You throw happiness, your most precious possession, away. The reward? You are absolved from living your life. You are absolved from defeat and rejection. No defeat, no rejection, can match the pain, defeat and rejection that you have already handed out to yourself.

This is a harrowing picture, I know. Yet how many people do you know who, instead of living, bring disaster upon themselves/are consumed with guilt or worry/have very low self-esteem? For women, in particular (often because of lack of encouragement in childhood, the lack of parents who will constantly say, 'You can do it'), the question of self-worth and so self-confidence is critical. A woman told me recently, 'If a man said anything complimentary to me I'd think he was slightly potty, deluded.' Yet she was very attractive. What she said revealed her very low opinion of herself.

Guilt is the mischief-maker in all this, so how do we get rid of it? At one time, for many people, the Church and a religious faith took care of the matter. If a person committed a sin (and you can only commit a sin if you believe in God), the priest could impose a penance and absolve the person from sin, wipe the slate clean, deal with the guilt. Confession was, it was held, good for the soul. The sinner, still loved by God, could start again with a clean sheet. It was Jesus who took the weight. He died to save our souls and to save us from sin (and absolve us from guilt).

In a secular society (in which less than 10 per cent of the population regularly attend church), guilt is not so regularly or effectively dealt with. When you have done something wrong you may carry your feelings of guilt around with you for a very long time. Your self-imposed penance *could* be a very harsh one indeed. God, via the priest, can forgive us. It is rarely so simple for us to forgive ourselves.

Let me assume you have a problem. Let me assume (and this is a big assumption) that you really want to solve it. There are a number of sensible, logical things you can do. You could go to your GP and talk about it. If you're desperate, depressed, suicidal, you could ring The Samaritans (their telephone number will be in your telephone book) and, again, talk to somebody. It's always better to talk about a painful problem than to keep it to ourselves. Those helpers know about Pain. Some of them have been there, know the place themselves.

You could go to your Citizens' Advice Bureau (CAB) and ask for the address of a local women's support group, a group for expectant single mothers, a good counsellor. You could ask what advice and support there is in your area for gays, the unemployed, those who have to look after an aged parent, whatever your concern may be. The CAB will give you advice, both free and confidential, on money and tax matters, separation, divorce, unwanted pregnancy. They can provide an address for you to contact no matter how intimate and distressing your problem is.

If your problem is one of the heart you could write to an agony aunt or uncle about it (or talk to a good friend). If you're over-dependent on your love for someone, you could join an evening class, a group, to take up new interests, widen your horizons, meet new people so that you become more self-reliant and don't have all your emotional eggs in one basket. Whatever your problem is there is always support available somewhere in the community. People do care; people are learning to help each other.

Then why, in the face of all this available help, do people still suffer so much emotional pain? I think it is because: (a) they want to cling to the problem; (b) they want a solution which will make sombody else do the work; (c) they want an easy solution, a magic helper who will wave a wand and the problem will disappear. What many people want is somebody they can pass the parcel on to, hand over their heavy load of miseries accrued from the past and say, in effect, 'Here. You take responsibility. I'm tired of trying to be me. Would you kindly be me for me or, at least, look after me like a child so that I don't have to take responsibility for myself and make any real decisions.'

This seems a harsh view but I see it happening all around me: women, the flag of the Cinderella complex unfurled, looking for the Handsome Prince who will solve all their troubles; men, Oedipus complex alive and well, looking not for a woman to care for, share with, co-exist in love and as *real* people, but for a mother who will look after him and provide for his physical and emotional needs; men and women who act out strange plays in which the sack of negative emotions from the past is dumped on

24

each other's knee in turn. There are no easy solutions to life's problems. This doesn't prevent people from looking for them, eschewing the notion that the solutions, whether complete or the best possible, lie in our own hands. We are the captains of our fate, not Captain Marvellous/the Handsome Prince/Big Nurse/ Mother Substitute. To realize that we are responsible for our own happiness, and that we throw it away at our own volition, is the beginning of wisdom. To realize this is to get to the starting line. It is surprising how many of us remain in the paddock desperately seeking a magic helper who will solve all our problems.

By magic helper I don't mean God (I have no intention of insulting those of a religious persuasion); God, as I understand it, helps those who help themselves. I don't mean professional therapists, though sometimes therapy can help us cope better with life.

In her book *Talking to a Stranger: a Consumer's Guide to Therapy* (Fontana Original) Lindsay Knight discusses the different types of therapy now available. She describes how these therapies work, the pros and cons of each and whether they're available on the NHS (and, if they're not, how much they cost). There's a chapter on 'How to Find a Therapist' and a useful list of addresses. It's a very helpful book for anybody who thinks that therapy may help to give them the guidance and insight they need to solve their problems. It *can* help to talk over our problems with a stranger.

What doesn't help is insight without action, a belief that somebody else will wipe away your tears, provide an instant cure. Somebody once asked Woody Allen how his analysis was going (after twenty years). 'Slowly,' said W.A. The aim of therapy is not to cure you. It is not, as Freud rather depressingly once said, to turn neurotic misery into ordinary unhappiness. It is simply to enable you to make choices rather than to drift along on a less-than-magic carpet, never knowing where to land.

Therapy has its limitations. The therapist has his/her defined role but, at the end of the day, it is you that has to come to a decision. That takes courage. Where the therapy leads on to the requisite decisiveness and courage I consider it to be time well spent. Therapy can provide insight; but it cannot actually solve the problem. Consider the following two life situations:

Case 1. I love only you. X and Y are married but not to each other. She's 41, he's 50. They love each other passionately but he won't leave his wife and children (aged 18, 22 and 24) to marry her. They've been having an affair for six years, meeting at weekends. 'If he married me,' says X, 'we'd have two happy people instead of four miserable ones.' He loves her but he also loves the comforts of his home. He's also getting something from each of his two worlds. She's miserable. *He* can put up with it.

What is the solution to X's misery? She desperately wants to marry Y. Should she consult a therapist? How would that help? It may clarify issues (but so would a chat to a trusted friend in a pub). The therapist cannot arrange a marriage. All he/she can do is to point out the choices: (a) stay as you are and enjoy the weekends (and keep hoping); (b) give up Y and put an end to your emotional conflict. Either way, it's going to be painful for X. All she has to decide is which sort of pain she prefers, which course of action will be better for her. There just is no perfect solution to her problem if Y insists he won't marry her.

Case 2. The money box. Aurelia has a well-paid job in a large department store. Her husband is a potter and has recently started his own business consisting of a small shop and a pottery on the premises. 'The trouble is,' says Aurelia, 'he's losing money hand over fist.' The husband claims that he's an artist and that money is unimportant to him. They live in a pleasant house and dine out once a week. The business, house and the meals are all paid for by Aurelia.

'I'm starting to resent it deeply,' she says. 'I'm also beginning to dislike my husband intensely. He just runs away from financial responsibility, leaves it all to me.' Aurelia's job, as a buyer, takes her away from home for a great deal of the time. That alleviates the problem (and she has a lover whom she meets regularly), but it doesn't solve the problem. Her husband is still there when she goes home. Her resentment of and bitterness at his behaviour are with her all of the time.

What's the answer? I leave you to come up with the choices that Aurelia has and to decide for yourself what would be the best course of action. I merely want to illustrate that mental conflict is about the whole person, about total (often quite awful) situations that people find themselves in. There is no rapid cure, no pills the patient can take to bring quick relief. There is only a choice to be made, deeds to be done, *by the person who is suffering*.

26

One woman in Ms Knight's book reports that therapy for her was 'a succession of rather pathetic little discoveries about oneself, coming to terms with a series of losses'. That's fine; that's dealing with unfinished business; that's learning to look at, and accept, defeat, loss, pain from the past. As Craig Raine says, 'It is the onion memory that makes me cry.' I am all for strolls down memory lane when they give us hope and meaning and courage to find the main road of life again.

Therapy, and it goes on in pubs, in night classes, in all sorts of places where people, as friends, are gathered together, is a journey undertaken to find an enjoyable route, a new path, a better way of life. It is to do with the secret places of the heart, with shining a torch in those secret places. It is the grief that doesn't speak that causes us most pain. We need to learn to talk about our pain. To whom we talk is up to us. We must all learn to bring our pain into the open.

I hope you won't look for magic helpers but real helpers. I hope you won't expect easy solutions. It may work with measles or a sore throat, but it doesn't work with human emotions. There is no instant cure for heartache.

I sincerely believe we can be who we want to be. We have choice. Choosing isn't easy and some of us never make any real choices in our whole lives. To choose you have to have courage. To choose you have to face the past, look it straight in the eye and say, 'What was, was.' Then, you are at liberty to say, 'What is, is.' What is, is choice and freedom.

These are the points to remember:

1   *There are people who will help.* There is no magic helper.
2   *There is no fairy-tale castle where, once inside, all your problems cease.* You can't solve your problems by closing your eyes until they go away. You can only work out strategies that really tackle the problem and set you on the road towards peace of mind.
3   *Guilt solves nothing.* Guilt is a useless emotion, and so is worry. It is *always* better to do something about a problem than to sit there worrying about it, or feeling guilty.
4   *There are no quick cures in mental life.* None of us change from a caterpillar into a butterfly in a day. It takes time. It is a step-by-step journey towards competence and self-confidence. The most important step is the first, talking about the problem, finding help. That first step takes the most courage.

5 *Don't have unreal expectations*. Nobody is happy all the time. Learn to cope (and to snatch those moments of happiness when they come along, if possible with a loud cry of, 'I deserve this!')

6 *It takes an enormous amount of energy to keep undesirable thoughts or emotions repressed*. This is why so many people are tired all of the time, trying desperately to keep the lid on the id. Get your thoughts out, talk about them. Talking helps, especially when it is talking about how you *feel*.

7 *Take some risks*. Pay the price of anxiety. How can you grow as a person, and gain confidence, if you don't take *some* risks? Life *is* risky. Don't play it absolutely safe all of the time.

8 *We're all dependent on others (even if it's only the milkman or postman)*. That doesn't mean you have to sign over your emotional life to somebody else. Real love is caring, sharing and having fun together, as equals. It isn't the abnegation of responsibility for yourself, or saying to somebody, 'Take me. I'm yours. Look after me so that I'll never have to make another decision again, ever.' That's silliness, not love.

9 *If you can't get what you want get what you need*. I can't have everything I want. Neither can you. There *are* things I need and I'm willing to put myself out to get them. I hope you are too. Get your priorities in order and go for those things that really mean something to you.

10 *The past is over*. What was, was. Don't keep turning back to it. The starting line is always NOW. What is, is. Learn to accept yourself and to deal with today. That's a very big step indeed towards coping and self-fulfilment.

Chapter 3
Attitude is all

It is not what happens to you that is important. What is important is your attitude towards it. It is not the event but your reaction to the event. I believe that human beings have some say in the outcome of their lives. I believe I have problems to face, choices to make. I tell the story of my own life and it is not being written for me. *Nothing is predetermined* and at every stage of my life I have choices to make. The choices I make will determine which further choices are available to me.

I'm saying this because, at one time, I used to believe that a large part of an adult's life was determined by what had happened to him/her during childhood. I was once a Freudian. Now, I am an eclectic, simply using those parts of any psychological theory which I find useful. I still think that Freud was a great and courageous man. I doubt whether his theories concerning human behaviour are correct.

Freud altered the way in which human beings see themselves. Galileo had shown that the earth was not the centre of the universe; Darwin had suggested that human beings were descended from apes, not angels; Freud put forward the view that the actions of men and women are unconsciously motivated and that this motivation is emotional rather than rational. Reason, as the basis of human behaviour, was dethroned.

There is no doubt, as far as I'm concerned, that the unconscious mind exists. There is the evidence of dreams, of hypnosis. There are slips of the pen and of the tongue. There are those 'forgotten' dental appointments and memories which are stored for years and *do* affect behaviour. I used to work in the next room to a hypnotist. If his patient wasn't asleep by the count of ten he would shout, 'Go to sleep, you b . . . ' The next sounds emanating from the patient's mouth would be a baby's cry or the voice of a 3-year-old demanding to play with the toys.

I can see the unconscious mind at work in the lives of people. X marries (four times, to date) the most unsuitable women; Y marries someone who looks, and behaves, exactly like his mother; Z invariably attracts violent men, who abuse her, mistreat her, leave her; A has to argue, to quarrel, to provoke a terrible scene, before she can make love; B can only make love to women who wear a nanny's or nurse's uniform. Some people's lives *are* like a tape recording which is played again and again and again. There is a pattern to their lives and it isn't one that leads to self-fulfilment and happiness.

This is a bleak scenario and it is one in which I firmly believed when I was a teenager (which was when I first read Freud). The mind was like an iceberg, one-sixth of which (the conscious mind) was above water. The rest (the unconscious) was submerged. This was the gimmee-gimmee, 'I want it now', irrational, emotional part of the mind which knew nothing of time and space, obeyed no logic and wanted immediate gratification. The id, that vast unknown territory, was governed by the Pleasure Principle and paid no heed to the demands of reality.

Within each of us (so Freud claimed) a titanic battle is fought between the id and the ego (aided by the super-ego). The super-ego consists of serried ranks of injunctions and prohibitions — 'Don't do that'; 'Mummy doesn't like that' — which we carry about with us from childhood. The mental conflict can only be ended if the ego secures a victory. 'Where id was,' said Freud, 'there shall be ego.'

I was, when young, very taken with this model of the human mind. I used to draw, in my exercise books, models of my own: the mind as a boiling-pan with a lid on. (The contents of the pan, boiling away merrily, were the id; the lid of the pan, bouncing up and down under the pressure, was the ego.)

I thought then (and still do) that Freud's description of defence mechanisms was useful. I've observed, through the years, how people project their feelings on to other people, how people deny their feelings, intellectualize them, talk about the problem rather than feeling it (and doing something about it). I've seen, in therapy, how people identify with the therapist and/or transfer their hostile/loving impulses on to him/her. I've seen how children take on board the good and the bad of their own parents and sometimes live out the fantasies and dreams of a parent. I've seen, too, how some people spend years repressing their feelings and how others manage to sublimate those feelings and convert the psychic energy into creative outlets.

For Freud the first five years of life were crucial. There were three stages of psychological development during these years: oral, anal and oedipal. An adult could reveal, according to Freud, a fixation on any one of these stages. To Freudians, a person who smokes is fixated at the oral stage, as are very heavy drinkers. Somebody who is overly tidy − or who goes in for collecting things − is fixated at the anal stage. A person fixated at the oedipal stage will choose a partner who reminds him/her of the parent of the opposite sex.

In 1910, Freud wrote to Carl Jung: 'My dear Jung, promise me never to abandon the sexual theory. That is the most essential thing of all. You see we must make a dogma of it, an unshakeable bulwark.' For Freud the early sexual experiences of the child formed the character. The central influence in the development of personality *was the primal sexual attraction of the child for the parent of the opposite sex.*

Freud perceived the link between repressed childhood experiences (buried in the unconscious) and the adult fears, anxieties, neuroses, panics and phobias that afflicted his patients. He believed that if the childhood emotions could be drawn back to the surface, talked about and analysed, their power to have such detrimental effects in the lives of adults would be neutralized. For Freud those early experiences were vital. Psychic processes are strictly determined. We don't do what we do because we want to; we do as we do because we must. It is not a very optimistic view of human nature. It emphasizes not choice, but inevitability.

It is possible that Freud's theories reveal more about Sigmund Freud than they do about human behaviour? He was dominated by a slender, attractive, intelligent mother (who was 21 when Freud was born and who lived to be 95). Freud's father, Jakob, was twice his wife's age (he was 51 when Sigmund was 10). Freud's theories, especially the Oedipus complex, could be inextricably linked with his own childhood.

Sigmund Freud, as a child and a man, was extremely isolated. His later theories reflect his narcissism and his loneliness: men and women, adrift on the ocean of life, haunted by the injunctions of the super-ego, tossed by the storms of the id, with only a frail ego to give them courage in the face of their isolation. His first piece of research was on the sex life of eels. He was, for a young man with five sisters, curiously prudish in his attitude to sex. For the most part he saw this important human

31

function as being for procreation, not pleasure, and the insistence of today's women on their own sexuality — the ownership of their own bodies — would have deeply shocked him. It is odd that Freud, to the general public, is associated with sex, when, in reality, Freud was a prude. His letters to his fiancée, Martha Bernays, are strikingly reminiscent of mine to the milkman.

I began to wonder about Freud. He says the id is the source of human destructiveness, yet it is also the source of human creativeness; we can do nothing without the energy it supplies. The energy has to be harnessed to good effect, rather than dampened down. Also Freud was largely ignorant of mass neurosis and group dynamics — group psychology was not his *métier*. He was a lonely child and a dreamer. It is no accident that his greatest work is *The Interpretation of Dreams*. None of his ideas were tested in varying communities, different classes. Freud had few women colleagues. He once asked one woman colleague, Marie Bonaparte, 'What do women *want*?' He was genuinely puzzled by women but, then, he was a man, a Jew, a member of the European bourgeoisie and highly patriarchal. Freud was interested in his patients, not people. Freud distrusted what Ernest Jones called 'the average mind'. Freud's study was full of precious objects. Each day Freud's personal barber would come to trim the master's beard. Freud was not a man of the people. He was a nineteenth-century patriarch who distrusted democracy and his theories were tested out on a small sample of middle-aged Viennese ladies. That doesn't disprove them but it hardly gives them scientific credence.

As a student, I became more and more interested in the work of Carl Jung. Jung's childhood was the opposite of Freud's in that he loved his father (a weak but likeable man) and was highly ambivalent towards his mother (a dominant and highly neurotic woman). Jung's mother was outgoing, 'problematical and inconsistent'. His father, a pastor in the Calvinist Reformed Church of Switzerland, was introverted and depressed, a once-holy man who had lost his self-confidence, and his faith.

Freud's psychology was shot through with paternalism. Jungian psychology is rooted in the maternal: it is concerned with the search for self and obsessed with images of Woman as devourer and destroyer as well as nurturer and protector.

Jung was not so much concerned with the super-ego (or repression) as with the efforts of the developing personality to extricate itself from 'the toils of maternal encirclement'. Like Freud, Jung was a lonely child. He claimed that the most important experiences of his life came to him when he was alone. His autobiography contains very little about personal relationships; his wife, for example, is hardly mentioned. His only comment on her death is, 'After my wife's death in 1955, I felt an inner obligation to become what I myself am.'

Perhaps because he was reared in the Swiss countryside, Jung had a far more relaxed attitude towards sex than Freud. His rural childhood helped him to see sex as an integral part of life's pattern of birth, procreation and death. 'Sex,' said Jung, 'is a playground for lonely scientists.' Freud interpreted all emotionally significant experience as derived from sex. For Jung, sex was symbolic. It could possess a 'numinous' quality and could lead to a union of opposites and wholeness.

For Freud, the physical, the *symptom*, was vital. (If you went to Freud and couldn't produce a symptom, told him that you were unhappy, he would, unlike Jung, turn you away.) For Freud, a person's life was determined by what had gone before. For Jung, the spiritual was of supreme importance and life was an unfolding pattern, with both eyes fixed firmly on what was yet to be. We 'come to a standstill' or 'get stuck' *in the present* (rather than fixated on the past). This 'getting stuck' is the theme of all those fairy stories with a locked door to which the heroine (or hero) must find the key in order to enter the enchanted garden.

Freud, the sceptic, and Jung, the mystic, travelled along very different roads. Freud's determinism meant we had little choice: the emotional crop we sow in childhood, we reap as adults. Jung travelled in hope. His theories were teleological. He believed that our behaviour is affected by our future aims. Freud was an atheist. Jung, when John Freeman asked him on television (in his *Face to Face* interview in 1959) whether he believed in God, said, 'Difficult to answer. I *know*. I don't need to believe.' Jung died in 1961; on the day of his death there was a tremendous storm over the lake at Zurich, at the edge of which Jung lived. To me, this is a particularly pleasing example of the pathetic fallacy. Jung would have accepted it as appropriate. Over his front door was carved the inscription: '*Vocatus atque non vocatus deus aderit*' (Invoked or not the god will be present). Freud died, in 1939, in London of cancer of the throat, an atheist to the last.

33

All of Jung's work may be seen as an attempt to build a religious scaffolding to repair life's shabby edifices and to gain, within himself, that sure conviction of God, that unshakeable faith, that had once sustained his own father. Jung acknowledges the darker, more primitive side of the human personality. This shadier, unconscious region of the mind Jung calls 'the shadow'. It contains our instincts, our emotional energy, our animal spirits. Like the id, it is a force for evil, or good. It has to be channelled. If it is totally suppressed we lose our spontaneity, creativity, vivid insights, joyousness, wisdom, passion. When the self accepts the shadow and is no longer frightened by it, then the personality becomes more alive and vigorous, both physically and mentally.

The 'persona' is another part of the personality: the mask you present to the world. (A *persona* was the Roman actor's mask.) Your persona is the role you play, the person you wish to present, the person you wish others to see. Where the persona is tied securely to the self — springs from the self — all is well. If the persona becomes detached from the solid ground of the true self disintegration and tragedy can result. In Arthur Miller's *Death of a Salesman*, Willy Loman's role as super-salesman so dominates his life that he forgets who he is, or could be. It's rather as Voltaire said, 'It is a pity to be born a man and die a grocer.'

For Jung the 'self' is the focus of the mind. It includes consciousness and unconsciousness. The integration of the different elements of the mind into a consistent, esteemed self is the major task of life. A part of the unconscious mind is the 'collective unconscious' which contains various stock characters on the stage of human experience including the Witch, the Mother, the Good Fairy, the Good Father, the Devil. Also present are the 'anima' (a man's image of a woman) and the 'animus' (a woman's image of a man).

In order to become real people, women must accept and assimilate the animus (ie, the masculine components) within them. Men must incorporate the anima (the more feminine, tender side of their natures). When a man is able to give love, feel love, to be gentle, he is most truly a man. Women must accept the masculine component within them or they become false, shallow 'candy floss' females. Too much animus, however, can make women belligerent and aggressive. For Jung the emphasis was always on harmony and balance between the various parts of the mind. This inner harmony Jung called 'individuation'.

I found Jung's theories attractive as a young student. (Although I didn't agree with his theory of 'psychological types' nor of his division of people into 'introverts' and 'extroverts'; most of us are a mixture of both and a great deal depends on who we are with, and what day of the week it is, as to whether we're withdrawn or outgoing.) It still seems to me that, unless Mankind is about to enter a spiritual dark ages, there *is* more to life than bread alone and that life is a great deal more than the physical world (and determinism). In my view, people do have spiritual yearning and have a need for a meaning in their lives. Jung took cognizance of that yearning, and that need.

As a student, I had read very little of Alfred Adler. I knew him to be, together with Freud and Jung, one of the 'Big Three' of psychology but had regarded him as a minor figure. In my first job after university, I worked with Dr Bierer, who had worked with Adler and who was a committed and distinguished Adlerian. It was then that I learned how useful, and inspiring, many of Adler's ideas are.

For both Freud and Jung the group and the community were of minor significance compared to the individual. It is Adler who gives due weight to group psychology and to the way in which we react, in the here and now, to other people. Adler's background is very different from Freud's. He was a friendly, witty and urbane man who was born in Vienna, the second of six children. He had a father who was forceful and attractive, a mother who was nervous and moody. As a child Adler overheard the family doctor tell his mother that he (Alfred) didn't have very long to live. It was this that made him choose medicine as a career!

Adler was an odd-looking man with curious, moon-shaped features, and 'piggy' eyes (he bears a striking resemblance to Miss Piggy on 'The Muppet Show'). He was of small stature and very self-conscious. One of the central tenets of Adler's doctrine was that all life was movement: hopefully, from a minus to a plus. Adler was his father's favourite. He was less attached to his mother, who preferred the first born. This was the eldest son and a great rival of Alfred's. As an old man Adler complained that his older brother was 'still ahead of me'. Alfred's childhood was, on the face of it, idyllic. He was surrounded by a noisy, happy family but he developed (mainly through his relationship with his brother) the 'inferiority complex' that came to be part of his personality (and a central part of his theory).

What are the main ideas in Adlerian theory? To Freud's two criteria of mental health — to be able to work and to love: *lieben und arbeiten* — Adler added a third: the ability to form friendships. To avoid neurosis, 'social goals' must replace individual goals; the antidote to neurosis is *Gemeinschaftgefühl*, or community feeling. It is the Will to Power, not sex, which is the prime cause of human misery.

Adler explains, in his work, his notions of 'sibling rivalry' and how ordinal position in the family affects personality and how the neurotic compensates for real or imagined feelings of inferiority. 'To be a human being,' wrote Adler, 'means the possession of a feeling of inferiority that is constantly pressing on towards its own conquest.' Who could have understood better than Adler, with that favoured, 'mummy's boy' elder brother, the pain of sibling rivalry? Who knew so well, with his generous, loving personality, the harm that can come when human beings substitute the Will to Power for love?

Freud had emphasized loneliness, the intra-psychic war within individuals fighting alone against the incessant demands of the id. Adler reminds us that people live in groups and that it is in working together with others in mutually supportive social relationships that many people find comfort, solace, therapy. Other people can give us, if they respect us, happiness, self-respect, purpose. Nobody has to, or should, spend a whole lifetime looking in the mirror.

Men and women do not, usually, live alone. They are social animals. Alone, problems are magnified. With friendship and companionship, people see that they are not alone and that others have their problems too. This may be the road away from self-pity back to self-regard.

During my work with Bierer I saw a boy who was very withdrawn. He joined a club which Bierer had formed, which the lad attended in the evening, and there he met a girl. What that girl did for him I didn't know then and don't know now, but her effect on the lad was much more therapeutic than my sessions with him. In the community there are vast human resources. Therapy often consists of utilizing them, having the wisdom to see that what people need may not be analysis but companionship, comfort, love.

36

When I look back now on my clinic work, I can see that manipulating human situations (urging mother to find a part-time job, to help out at a playgroup, urging father to join a group or modify his work hours to spend more time with the children) was, and is, much more effective than fishing around in the id, trying to land the 'cause' of the problem. It is human contact, the provision of human warmth and solace, which many people need. It is the need for belongingness, the need to do something useful, which far outweighs the need to peer into the dark corners of their mind.

The healing power of friendship, learning to work for and alongside others, offers the best remedy for conflict and neurosis. What is the point in labelling that mother depressed, this father neurotic? It is what we *do* about it that counts. It is in the group, in the community that the best therapy is available: not in the clinic, being interminably analysed, giving fancy names to what is most of the time old-fashioned loneliness or unhappiness. The cure for 'dis-ease' lies, according to Adler, not in unravelling the ball of wool of somebody's early complexes, but rather in substituting new, more socially orientated goals in place of self-obsession (and self-aggrandizement).

Adler used to ask his patients, 'What would you do if you could walk out of here fit and well?' Most of the time it was the patient's neurotic life-style that was the cause of the dis-ease — striving for spurious goals, always attempting to compensate for some imagined inferiority.

The most vivid example of a warped life-style I ever encountered was a man who worked all day, every day in a high-powered executive job. He worried about the job and his performance in it and consequently developed a duodenal ulcer. His doctor advised him to change his job or off-load some of his responsibility, that he was leading a very stressful life. The result of the warning? He decided to have an operation for the ulcer and carried on with his work exactly as before. That is rigid, non-adaptive behaviour. It is behaviour which ranks health and happiness lower than being best, being No. 1, being 'indispensable'. How foolish.

What I liked about Adler's theories was that they were not, like Freud's, about the past; they were not, like Jung's, about the future; they were about *now*. In life, it is always the Here and Now, today, which is important. The past is a memory, tomorrow is only a dream, but today, well-lived, gives us hope

37

for tomorrow. It is the optimism, and hope, which is crucial to those who wish to get better, *be* better, improve the quality of their lives.

It also appears to me that many of the things that Adler says are true. Take ordinal position in the family: each child, according to position in the family, will have certain personality characteristics, a certain life-style. The second child, like Adler, and myself, will try to outdo the first; the third child will try to excel over the second. It is the middle children in the family who respond to rivalrous feelings most readily.

Here is what Adler says about first- and second-born children: 'I have regularly found that the first-born shows a conservative element in his attitude. He reckons with existing strength, makes pacts with power and shows a certain conciliatoriness. . . . The second-born finds another in front of, or next to him, who can do more, who means more, who has more freedom and who is superior to him. If the second-born is able to develop he will live in a constant state of tension in order to get ahead of the first-born.'

That was, is, true in my own life (having an older, much loved elder brother) and I suspect that sibling rivalry plays a large part in all our lives. Now, I don't dislike my brother, don't compare myself with him, but I do accept that I am pushy, competitive, striving. It's part of my nature. I have learned to live with it and accept it. The notion of sibling rivalry has been very useful in coming to understand other people's problems, especially as I have been there myself.

According to Adler, 'individual psychology' (the name given to Adlerian psychology) seeks to 'deepen the understanding of human nature which is to be done by understanding the relationship of the individual to his socially determined tasks . . . in the earliest days of childhood, the child, uncomprehendingly and mistakenly, forms a model, a goal and ideal, a life-plan, which, knowingly-unknowingly, it follows.'

This *Lebensziel*, or life-goal, has as its object 'perfection, superiority and god-like power', but runs into the demands of the family, the real world. So the child learns to manipulate, learns that the weak get as much attention, if not more, than the strong. Every symptom has a meaning, and being ill can be a concealed form of power. Being ill or neurotic, ie, not knowing what to choose, which way to jump, can have its own rewards. It can bring attention, sympathy. It can stave off the day when we have to make a decision to do something about our lives.

What Adler was saying, for me, was that pain was part of life; what counted was our reaction to it. Failure was part of life; perfection is yet another fictitious goal. Disappointment and grief are part of life; which is why we need courage. We need to look forward, not backward (as I stressed in Chapter 2). We need to look outward, not inward. Too much psychology and self-analysis can be damaging to your health. Life is about people, relationships. We must learn to reach out, not look in the mirror.

Failure is part of life, part of being a human being. What does it matter if you fail so long as you can say, 'I did my best'? We learn more from our failures than our triumphs, more from being willing to try than wanting to be the best. Failure is the best teacher − a harsh one, but the best. Why, like Freud, try to be No. 1 all the time? Co-operation is a much more vital principle in relationships than competition. Take responsibility for your failure, if it was your responsibility. Don't blame others. Then pat yourself on the back for having the courage to try and go out and live your life. You deserve it − for being courageous.

I am sure that Adler was right about power. It wasn't love that inspired Hitler, but his own sense of inferiority and his Will to Power. He turned Europe into his nursery and, like a cantankerous child, destroyed it. It isn't love, or lack of it, that motivates neurotics; it's the wish for attention and power. It isn't love, or lack of it, that destroys families; it is the struggle for power that takes place within them. The solution? To learn to co-operate, work together, share. Equality, justice, works the same in the family as it does in society, works the same whether we are talking about our own personal relationships or about women's lib., gay rights, opportunities for ethnic minorities or British industry. Co-operation is the way forward. To want to be superior is the way to disaster.

Adler's was the psychology of common sense. What most people want when they have a problem is someone to talk to, someone who will help them to clarify the issues, deal with their feelings, make choices. That person can be a psychologist, a lawyer, a social worker, a good friend. What people don't need is an excavation of their infantile neuroses, an exploration of their childhood sexuality.

I once met a famous film star who told me that she was undergoing psychoanalysis. I asked her why and she said, 'It helps me to understand myself a little more.' That seemed to me a perfectly good answer (and she could afford the cost of the treatment). There are quicker ways to self-understanding and, moreover, insight, by itself, solves nothing. In the beginning was the deed. To get to the deed, most people want comfort, solace, understanding. Then, they must take the first step to getting themselves better. Freud is a luxury; psychoanalysis *may* improve the quality of your life but it's a long way round to see the tasks that confront you. It's an indulgence that most of us can't afford.

I have learned, from Adler, that what counts in life is attitude. I have learned not to want to be No. 1 all the time. I have learned that co-operation and community feeling *is* the antidote to neurosis. I have learned that life is about courage, not infantile sexuality.

Like Jung, I have my doubts about the importance of sex in human affairs. Sex is a way in which we show our need for contact comfort, for belonging, for being cherished, but sex without love can be a very lonely business and one in which the Will to Power operates, making the participants feel even more lonely, abandoned and alienated. Sex may have been important to Freud's patients; to whom it may not have been available. Now that it is available we know it's limitations. Love is vital, a Ruling Principle. Sex isn't. It should be, like our other human activities, suffused with sharing, caring and love.

How, then, do we use psychological theory to help us to cope, and to grow as human beings? We try to hammer out a positive philosophy of life, stressing the present rather than the past or the future. We use grief and pain as an opportunity to grow, learn something, move forward (and to give something back to our fellow human beings). We accept that bad times will come along, but have the courage to know that good times will come along (and to use what we learned during those bad times to help others).

We all have to learn to say, 'Win or lose, I'm going to give a good account of myself and do my best, come what may. I owe it to myself.' Few people had perfect childhoods. To live chained to the gate-post of the past is to live, at best, half a life. We have to learn to say:

I *am* imperfect.

I *am* neurotic. There are days when I cannot decide what to wear, what to eat, never mind how to live my life.

I *am* too short/tall, fat/thin, square/round.

I *am* weak. I need help, comfort, support.

I *am* a human being.

This puts us all on the same footing, all able to help each other. It doesn't make me better than you. You have something to give; so do I. Together, we have tremendous resources. It's that feeling of belonging to the human race, with all its imperfections, that's so important.

One of Freud's contemporaries was a neurologist called Dr Paul Moebius who had written a book called *On The Natural Feeble-Mindedness of Women*. Freud had the book in his personal library and I think that says a great deal about him. To have that attitude towards half of the human race is not a good augury when it comes to solving problems of human relationships. Perhaps Freud should have stayed with eels. They, at least, expected very little in the way of human contact and conversation. Unlike Freud's patients and sisters, they were probably happy that he should sit there making notes on their imperfections.

In life, the road is wider than long and the road can widen at every turn. At any time in our lives you and I can restructure our experience, see it in a different way, so that we benefit from our setbacks rather than being defeated by them. What happens to us *is* less important than what we make of it.

I am not going to give you ten tips at the end of this chapter. I am going to ask you ten questions. If you think about them, and answer them honestly, they may help you to gain some insight into your own life-style and, more importantly, move towards co-operation rather than needing to win all the time. As Adler said, life is movement, moving from a minus to a plus. The real plus is a concern for other people, that community feeling which Adler considered to be the road to mental health.

1   Do you do things for other people?
2   Do you do them for free, gratis and for nothing or are you paid for it?
3   What are your life goals? Are they goals you've worked out for yourself or 'better than' goals? Are you competing

against others or against yourself, being the best you can be?

4   What is your earliest memory? Does it feature a particular person? What did you think about that person then? What do you think about that person now? Has there been any change, any movement, in your attitude?

5   What is your ordinal position in the family you were born in? Were you a first, second, third child (or a fourth or fifth)? How do you think this affects your view of the world, and of other people?

6   Are you dominated by habit? Do you ever do anything different, anything new? Do you ever alter the way, or the order, in which you do things? Does change frighten you?

7   Do you belong to any groups? How often do you attend them? What friendships have you made in those groups and what do those friendships mean to you?

8   Do you think you had an unhappy childhood? How does your childhood compare with that of the people you know?

9   Do you see life as a battle? Against whom? Against what? What is your definition of success, of winning that battle?

10   Which is more important − insight or action? What steps have you taken recently to join a group, do something in the community or solve your own problems by helping other people with theirs? Do you consider yourself a co-operative person? In what way do you show that co-operation?

A friend of mine has a saying: 'Never put off until tomorrow what you can do the day after.' This is fine, if you want a quiet life, or want to avoid problems. To really live − and life is for living − you have to remember that in the beginning was the word and the word was: 'Act'. The time for action is always *now*. Don't worry about failure. There is none. There is only doing our best. I wish you what Alfred Adler would have wished you: I wish you courage.

Chapter 4
The enemy within: negative feelings

You may feel that I put too much stress on the emotions, on In Here rather than Out There. What about the terrible things that happen to people, you may ask; those times when life's slings and arrows really do fall thick and fast upon your head? 'When sorrows come,' says Hamlet, 'they come not single spies,/ But in battalions.' You may be going through an awful time — bereavement, a divorce, separation, financial difficulties, problems with the children — and you won't need me to tell you how it feels to be in *that* situation. You feel ghastly and must endure a patch in your life when it is genuinely very difficult to cope.

I cannot argue that life is just. It manifestly is not. Bad things, as I've said, happen to good people. You, like me, will know of people who have suffered the most appalling tragedy and, having thought about it — and the people concerned — you will have concluded, 'That's wrong. They were good people. He/she/they didn't deserve it.' I won't contradict you. All I can say, with truth, is that what was, was. The Moving Finger writes; and, having writ,/Moves on. You are left to decipher what has happened. You are left, in pain and suffering, to deal with Today. What is, is.

I believe that the worst thing that can happen to you in life is to be hit by a No. 72 bus. It needn't be a No. 72, it can come from any direction. Sometimes, you may just *feel* as though you've been hit by a bus. You haven't; you are still alive; you feel half-dead, numbed, shocked, depressed, harassed, unable to cope. Those feelings are *real*, whatever the event that triggered them off.

This is one reason why I'm against those lists of 'stressors', where the possible changes in your life are arranged according to the degree of stress involved, in a similar manner to a football league table. At the top of the league comes death of a spouse, followed by divorce, marital separation, prison sentence, death of a close family member, marriage(!), being fired from your job. At the bottom of the league are family get-togethers, holidays(!) and − believe it or not − Christmas.

I'm not convinced 'stressors' work in such a predictable way. There is always a subjective element to stress: your situation at that time, how you react to what's happened to you, what you make of it, how you construe it. Most people find divorce quite traumatic. I know several people, however, who went through a divorce calmly, with reason and dignity and very little stress. 'We both knew it was over,' one ex-wife said to me. 'We discussed it over supper one evening. That weekend, he moved out. We don't see each other any more but I bear no animosity towards him. It was just a mistake *on both our parts*.' They did not have any children.

Christmas, for some people, is a magic time, a family time. What if you have no family? What about children who live in residential homes, young people living alone, elderly people with no family to go to, no relatives living near by? Christmas, for some, can be an endurance test: a very stressful time indeed. What's sauce for the goose may not be sauce for grandma.

What I've always been dubious about when counselling people under stress is a grass is sparser in the next field approach: telling them that there is someone worse off than themselves. I don't think that helps. If you are at screaming pitch because your mother has come to stay for three months/ you have builders in and the noise and racket is driving you mad, does it really help for me to tell you that other people are coping with far worse things than you?

I doubt it. What you want to hear is something useful. I could perhaps suggest ways in which you can get out of the house, dilute your exposure to your mother/those builders. It's no use me saying to you, 'Life isn't easy.' You know that. You want to know what to do.

Some years ago I counselled a woman who intensely disliked her own mother, couldn't cope with contact with her and felt guilty about it. 'I'll ring her up,' my patient said, 'and she'll say, "Oh, it's you. Long time no hear. I thought you'd left the country" and I'll feel really put down even before I've said hello.' I advised her to meet her mother once a month, for lunch, and to be totally lovely towards her mother during that time (about an hour and a half). She could cope with this. It also helped to alleviate her guilt and to feel she had *some* control over the situation.

What I didn't say to her was, 'Some people have mothers much worse than yours. Some people have really dreadful mothers.' That might be true, but it wasn't what she was feeling. What she was feeling was that her relationship with her mother was eroding the rest of her life, depressing her, lowering her worth and that's what had to be dealt with. Comparisons, in terms of stressful situations, are odious. Stress is subjective. What you may be able to manage, I may find quite traumatic. Your challenge may be my downfall.

Later I will be talking about Out There and those awful events that befall us. Now, I want to continue to concentrate on feelings and talk not about luck, chance, bad fortune, fate, but about how you handle those negative emotions and how to conquer them. In the sphere of the intellect, in scientific knowledge, men and women have made giant strides since the days of the ancient Greeks. The Greeks could not land a man on the moon, build an aeroplane, make a laser beam. In the sphere of the emotions, however, they were just as sophisticated as us. There has been very little advance in the last two thousand years in the realm of feelings, of the human heart. Emotional conflict is still as prevalent − and painful − as it ever was. There are as many broken hearts now as there were in the days of Socrates and Plato.

What can you do about your emotions, the destructive or negative ones within you that prevent you from making the most of your life? Adler said that we have to turn a negative into a positive, so I want to look at some negative emotions to see how to cope better with what happens. Let's have a closer look at some of those enemies within, starting with *anger*.

Here is a letter written to 'On The Couch', my monthly column in the magazine *Cosmopolitan*:

'I have an automatic defence mechanism in the form of aggression. So far it's only verbal, but sometimes I get so angry I feel I could explode. I don't, though. Instead, I get panicky and become rude and horribly hostile, usually without provocation.

'I also indulge in self-pity, with all my energy being used to dwell on the fact that I have no friends and that I'm alone all the time. Yet, if people ask me to go out, I make excuses because I'm too apathetic to make the effort.

'I'm like two different people. At work, I'm energetic, outgoing and confident (I'm a nurse). My colleagues wouldn't recognize me outside work. Why am I angry all the time? Please help me to help myself.'

Here is a summary of my answer to 'Horribly Hostile'. It isn't a mortal sin to be angry. It's OK to express anger, not against some innocent person, but with the right person, at the right time and to the right extent. That's better than putting your anger on a back burner, letting it stew inside of you. Anger *can* be a way of pushing forward to positive change.

The *Oxford English Dictionary* defines anger as 'extreme displeasure' but, often, anger isn't extreme. We can be angry in a quiet way. Some people are silently angry all their lives. If you ask them why, they have no idea. They don't know it's all right to get annoyed once in a while. Anger is one of the sinews of the soul and if we never express it our soul atrophies and we become depressed.

The best thing to do with anger is to process it. When people asked Florence Nightingale what motivated her in her work she replied 'rage'. Rage against man's inhumanity to man – and woman. Lots of people start to live, and to become real people, as soon as they've learned to express (in positive ways) their justifiable anger.

You give without getting sufficient rewards in return. We all need *stroking*: little treats, appreciation, encouragement. You seem to get this in your work, but elsewhere you appear to be terribly lonely. At home, you sit there wallowing in self-pity and bubbling with rage. So express that anger within you: punch a pillow, pound the bed with a tennis racket, write a nasty letter to someone you're angry with (and don't send it). Write a letter to yourself and list all the things that make you feel fed up. Don't expect friends to treat you the same way as your patients. On the ward, you're the boss. Away from it, you're one of us and, with us, you're *allowed* to be angry from time to time.

So get out socially, meet more people. Don't get angry with them (they're neutral). Save your anger for poverty, disease, misery. Work through your resentments, have a good moan, complain (and let others have a moan too). *Stop* being hostile – reach out to people. Join a women's group, or start one up.

Join an evening class, take up a new interest. Let it lead to new adjustments, new pastures, new treats. We all need rewards.

Behind your anger should be love — love of yourself and of your needs. Direct your anger at the right targets. Be good to yourself and get that anger out of your system. The expression of righteous anger can be the beginning of growth, of development. Be you, be real, be angry when you want to be and (when you've had your say) don't forget to enjoy your life. Never let the sun set on your indignation. Better to express anger, make it work for you in a positive way, than to keep it bottled up inside you.

Anger comes, largely, from frustration. A simple model of anger is a child trying to build a tower of bricks. Things go wrong, the situation gets more and more fraught. Eventually, the child kicks down the tower and throws a tantrum. This happens with adults, too, though not with building blocks.

With adults, there is the same kind of accumulated frustration. Perhaps you've said yes to something when you'd meant to say no, so you feel annoyed with yourself. Next somebody 'puts you down', slights you, neglects you, treats you unfairly; that makes you feel more angry. Then things go wrong at home (or at work). Eventually, you can take no more. Something happens that triggers off an explosion of anger and you go berserk, start to rant and rave (and the nearest person collects the full force of your wrath). There's nothing rational — or fair — about anger.

The solution, of course, is to deal with the situations that make you angry *as they arise* (or at least the same day). This means that any dangerous accumulation of anger within you is avoided. Let's take two simple examples:

Case 1. Jo, aged 30. Jo is married, with two children. Her mother has treated her like a child for years and Jo resents this deeply; it makes her feel *very* angry. 'I'm a grown-up woman,' Jo says to me. 'Why does she talk to me as though I were six?' I tell Jo not to talk to me about it, but to have it out with her mother. Jo looks doubtful.

'My mother's ultra-sensitive,' she says. 'I don't think I'd dare to tell her.' I tell Jo that even a tortoise doesn't get anywhere unless he sticks his neck out. That weekend Jo rang me.

'I spoke to her,' she said. 'Amazing. She said she understood, she apologized and said she could see my point of view. Then we had a couple of sherries each and she kissed me before I left and said how proud she was of me. I'm dumbfounded.'

Why? The situation had been dealt with, brought into the open. How many people spend weeks/months/years seething with anger and rage simply because they won't say what they feel about a situation (or won't say NO)?

Case 2. John, aged 36. John has been with his company ten years. I meet John in a pub and he tells me that he feels he's underrated in his job, that he does good work for his boss and that he's under-valued and under-paid.

'Have you told the boss how you feel?' I ask John. 'No,' says John, looking at me in surprise. 'Why don't you?' I ask him. The following week he does. He's told that he's regarded as a key employee; he also gets his rise. 'I'd been smouldering about being under-valued in the job for the past two years,' says John. Some people can suppress anger for a week, others manage it for years. Occasionally, after a long, long simmering, it explodes into rage. Sometimes it is never expressed at all. To keep all that anger (which is emotional energy) locked up inside takes time and devotion. The bottling up of anger can detract from the quality of our lives and diminish our ability to cope with day-to-day living.

What about *rage*? You can, like Florence Nightingale, direct your rage against real injustice and evil in the world. You could, like a friend of mine, make a doll out of papier mâché and give it a hard time when you become unrestrainedly angry. ('Take that, you bastard,' you can hear her shouting in the kitchen when she's just come to the end of yet another disastrous love affair.) You can join a gym and work out your rage on the apparatus; you can, like Thomas Hardy, rage against the fates or, like Dylan Thomas, rage against the dying of the light.

You *shouldn't* take your rage out on innocent people (or the cat). They're not to blame for what's happening to you. You have to know who or what is making you feel like that and deal with that person/them/that situation, rather than project your rage on to those who happen to be nearest to you.

It isn't easy. I have a friend, a gentle giant of a man, 6′ 7″, who goes berserk twice a year. You can tell when the storm is coming and everybody within range gets out of the way. All hell breaks loose and then, about two hours later, he calms down. When you go back into the house there are things all over the floor, it looks like a bomb's hit the place. 'What do you get so angry about?' I've asked him. 'Life,' he says. He's not in the same bracket as Florence Nightingale in his conversion of anger into a plus (*and* he has to tidy up after his rage). Yet, he feels rage and that is his bi-annual way of expressing it.

You and I know what it's like to feel anger and rage. What has impressed me over the years is how men and women have learned to turn anger and rage to good effect. They have turned their attention to poverty in the world, to hunger, neglect, political oppression, suffering and misery. They have channelled their anger to help the physically and mentally handicapped, the elderly, the lonely, the suicidal, the confused. They have done work for children, and adults, in need of comfort. They have found comfort themselves by comforting others; they have helped themselves by helping others, or by fighting for something in which they strongly believed. The solution is In Here *and* Out There.

It is those who rage against the dying of the light in a way that helps others who turn anger to tenderness, rage to love, war to peace. You and I don't need to make a papier mâché doll or to argue with a neighbour (or our nearest and dearest) to get rid of the anger within us. There is injustice in the world and it is that which we must all rage against. Righteous anger can be the beginning of a meaningful, and happy, life.

Perhaps, of all the emotions, it is *jealousy* which reveals how psychic energy can be misdirected in ways which *can* be harmful, destructive — or even tragic — to the person concerned. There is enough suffering in the world without you inflicting it upon yourself. Jealousy is a wild thing, a monster, a giant baby with a rolling-pin. It comes through the door accompanied by fear of loss, hate and rage, envy, vulnerability and rage. It's a kind of madness. Somebody once told me that, when she was an infant, her older brother set fire to her pram — with her in it. *That's* jealousy.

I've visited this mad kingdom myself. When I was 8 years old I fell madly in love with Eleanor and we had an idyllic fortnight (in which I sent her love letters and she sent me loving glances). I gave her a rose and as I handed it to her the petals fell off it; I should have seen this as a sign that true love wouldn't run smooth. Two weeks later she rejected me for a suitor called Nigel who was, in modern parlance, a wimp.

My reaction to this A loves B but B loves C situation was to try to run Nigel down with my bike, repeatedly. I hated Nigel, much more than Salieri hated Mozart or Iago hated Othello. If there had been prizes for hate I would have won a large silver cup. Envy is coveting something (or someone) that somebody else has; jealousy is wanting something (or someone) that somebody else has *but you think belongs to you*. It's the feeling of being dispossessed (and that hurts). It's a feeling of having mummy, or daddy, all to yourself and somebody else coming along. That's when you reach for the matches.

Do I exaggerate? Consider the following cases:

Case A I'm in a pub with X. He thinks his wife is having an affair. He is angry, resentful and depressed. 'She's never wanted to go out in the evening by herself before,' he says. 'She's definitely meeting someone.' Notice the private logic. She could be (as a matter of fact, *is*) going to an evening class, but X doesn't want the facts. Jealousy is about *power and possession*. X wants his wife all to himself. When jealousy comes through the door, reason flies out of the window.

X told me that, one evening, his wife had come home with her hair in disarray. 'Maybe it was windy outside,' I said. X looked at me scornfully. As Iago says, 'Trifles light as air/ Are to the jealous confirmations strong/ As proofs of holy writ.' X became, over the months, more sad, bad and paranoid. His marriage is over now. When I say that jealousy is a monster, I don't exaggerate. His wife was seeing nobody. The Stranger was X. The Stranger had taken over his mind and had given him a chance to throw at his partner all that unfinished business of infancy. Twenty years of a good marriage was destroyed in one year of paranoid madness.

Case B J. tells me that she has seen her man with another woman, in a pub, talking and laughing together. 'So what?' I ask her. 'He's having an affair. I know he is,' she says. 'If he is having an affair, I'll leave him. I just couldn't take it, believe me.' I know J. I know about her rivalry with her younger sister when she was a child, and that's what's at the root of this, but her partner isn't having an affair: he tells me so himself, and I believe him.

Three months later the partnership is dead, buried. J. became quite irrational towards Y, her man: shouted at him, abused him, threw things at him. Eventually he walked out and *she forced it upon him*. It was her baby with the rolling-pin that

50

shattered their nest of love, it was the monster within her that forced her man away. Jealousy is murder and mayhem, grief and loss, a crazy world. Running Nigel down was nothing compared to what I've seen adults do to a loved one when they were smitten with jealousy.

As an agony uncle I receive hundreds of letters each year on the subject of jealousy. You may not like to think of yourself as capable of it, but you are. If you're particularly prone to possessiveness and jealousy, what can you do about it?

You should remember:

- *Jealousy is one of the most destructive and nasty emotions.* It can ruin your life and the lives of those around you. Have nothing to do with it.
- *Love is a privilege, not a possession.* If you love someone it is a risk, but your best bet — if you want him or her — is to offer respect and affection, not demand ownership.
- *Learn to trust.* What alternative have you got? Can you truly possess, own, another human being?
- *Regard feelings of jealousy as a warning sign.* Change is needed — *from you.* Look at the whole relationship. Talk about what you both need and want. If you do this, you still have a chance. Let the monster in and you're in trouble.
- *If you have a sister/brother, don't spend your life trying to beat her/him.* Why worry that she has a 22" waist or he has a BMW? Dance to the music of your own heart. Be the best possible you. Those feelings of rivalry, experienced as a child, must be recognized, faced up to, dealt with, or they will enter into your adult relationships and damage them.
- *Concentrate on you.* If he/she cheats, that is awful, but it is not the end of the relationship, unless you choose it to be. *Say* how you feel; discuss the situation; make your point. Then go out and develop your talents, interests, friendships. A love grows strong in the soil of trust, not possession.
- *Be strong with your unconscious.* Whenever the monster appears ring up central casting, complain. Jealousy, in my view, is inborn, but that doesn't mean you cannot control it. Look it straight in the eye. The one who gets hurt, with jealousy, is the one you love. It springs from your low self-esteem so make a few changes in your life and reach out, via trust and friendship, to love.

51

● *Don't project the nasties within you on to your partner.* To use your partner as an emotional punchbag, to take out on them your own problems and frustrations is grossly unfair.

Every adult human relationship is a contract between two people. Much of the time, what happens to a person in a relationship is what that person allows to happen. It's wise to look at the details of a contract before you sign on. I knew a woman who was engaged to a man for eight years. She was absolutely convinced that he would marry her eventually. He didn't. Instead he went off and married somebody else. Who was at fault? Should she have asked, 'What is the deal between the two of us?' It's better to know than to risk confusion, turmoil and the depression which suppressed anger brings in its wake.

It's amazing how women, in particular, will put up with situations that they didn't envisage. In a restaurant I once heard a woman order *tournedos*. The waiter brought her rump steak. 'It doesn't matter,' she said, 'I'll have it.' It doesn't matter? I think it does matter. If somebody is manipulating you, taking advantage of you, the answer is to get annoyed, get angry and speak your mind. Also, it has to be remembered that you are allowed to say no. Years ago, at school, I asked a girl called Susan to go out with me. She looked at me straight in the eye and said, 'No.' It's a useful word to remember in restaurants and in relationships.

Far more women than men suffer from *depression*. I think this depression results from suppressed anger. With love, God gives you the pieces: you have to decide which squares they go on. If a woman gives her love to a man who treats her badly she *is* going to become depressed and confused. She may be playing an elaborate game called 'Hurt Me, I Don't Deserve Anything Better'. More likely she just hasn't the self-confidence to look at him straight in the eye and say, 'This won't do.'

Taking charge of your emotions — and your life — means that (a) you have to face up to change; (b) you have to dip into the pool of human resources which surround you to find the sort of people who do have something to offer you. We underestimate other people; many of them are much kinder, more perceptive, than you think. Most of them know about pain and emotional distress. They've been there themselves.

The sort of people you need are those who can (a) reflect back your feeling and (b) encourage you to make the changes needed

52

for you to cope and make the move towards happiness. You need people who will tell you that you're not mad, that other people too have been depressed or frightened or in despair. You need people to say, 'Yes, I think you should do that' and 'Yes, you can do it. You can make it.' Encouragement is vital to human beings. You may be able to make changes in your life without using other people, but it is much easier when other people are there to listen to you, and give you those words of encouragement that mean so much.

Finding somebody to talk to about the way you feel, about your emotions, isn't an optional extra. It is a crucial step towards getting better. It is when In Here is confirmed, ratified by people Out There that you realize you're not the only one in that situation; that what you feel is real, valid and you are entitled to such feelings.

Consider depression. In mild cases the tried and trusted remedies of talking to a friend or a relative, having a break, going on holiday, having a change of scene, taking up a new hobby or interest may be all that is needed to lift the black cloud over your head. In serious cases of depression, when the Black Dog comes, when you walk down a dark tunnel with no light at the end, you will need to seek advice from your GP. You may need psychiatric counselling or anti-depressant drugs. Neither will, by themselves, cure depression.

The way out of the dark tunnel is by repeated contact with people who understand what is going on inside you and who will encourage you to take those tiny, first steps back to coping and happiness. It is in this way that Depressives Anonymous groups are so useful. The members of such groups know what it feels like to be depressed. That is why joining a therapy group of people with a variety of emotional problems helps too. At least, in the group, the depressive feels accepted. Those other members of the group know what pain feels like; that's why they're there.

So, with emotions, you have to beware of self-pity and sloth: a failure to say, 'Others can help me and I'm going to look for that help.' This isn't easy. Some people find it hard to admit they can't cope, find it hard to ask for help, think that they should cope with their own feelings or hold a situation together which is slowly, or quickly, falling apart.

A major mistake is to suppose that you ought to be braver, more adventurous, more daring than you are. I met an elderly lady on a train once. She asked me where I was going.

'Southend,' I said proudly. It was a big adventure for me; I was going from Dorset to Leigh-on-Sea to see my sister. 'Where are you going?' I asked her. 'Leningrad,' she said. She told me the story of her life; she was a very adventurous, brave person.

You may not be like that lady. You may be very shy and find it hard to go into a shop and ask for a newspaper. That's fine. That's you. You can learn to be a little bit more daring if you take it step by step, set the bar of adventurousness at a height to suit yourself. You'll have your own wants and needs; those things you'll want to change; those feelings inside yourself which you still haven't dealt with. If you feel spite, hate, rage, despair, jealousy and other negative emotions, there *is* something wrong. Erich Fromm said that destructiveness is the outcome of an unlived life. Those negative feelings *can* be very destructive.

So how do you cope with those feelings and start living your life? You have to learn that it's perfectly acceptable to say no when you want to. You have to learn to get rid of the clutter from your mind and to concentrate on what is important to you. You have to hold up those emotions where you can see them, name them, not be frightened of them. To do that you will probably need the help of others. It may be a good friend, or a relative, who helps. It may be a marriage guidance counsellor, a Samaritan, a doctor, a psychiatrist who helps. The help is there if you have the courage to take the first step and bring your problem out into the open.

You have many things to learn: how to make decisions, how to give yourself little rewards, how to plan your future rather than to simply agonize about it. You have to learn to ask, 'What is it *I* want?' It's not an easy question. It puts many people, especially those who like others to make decisions for them, on the spot.

You may find it helpful (some people do, some don't) to set yourself specific goals, to have *one* specific short-term goal and a specific long-term goal. What is useless is to say, 'Next year I intend to be a better person.' Set yourself a goal for the week, and make it one that you're reasonably confident of reaching. Having achieved it, reward yourself in some way. Then, set yourself a goal for the month; for instance, 'This month I will join an evening class or an aerobics group.' When you've achieved these sub-goals, make a goal for the year − and go for it.

Coping is reacting to external pressures, reacting to the situation, or other people. In some situations, such as when somebody in the family has a serious illness, all you may be able to do is cope (coping is better than non-coping). In those situations you must find people who will support you through the stressful time.

Coping, however, is not happiness. Happiness comes out of having a feeling that you have some say in your own life, are not just reacting to the environment but controlling it, and getting the rewards you seek. When you're happy you're more able to be content with your lot, or change things if you don't like it. Happiness is power. Happiness is being able to say, 'I feel OK. I am doing what I want to do and I can cope with change if change is necessary.'

To move from coping to happiness, from negative to positive feelings, there are certain strategies that have proved useful. They provide a way out from rage, anger, hate, envy, jealousy, depression and despair. They also provide the means of moving forward, towards a life that is lived rather than one which remains unlived. These strategies are:

1 *Accept you have a problem (if you have) and talk about it, to the person concerned and/or to others who can give friendly or professional advice*. A famous actor, on stage, declaimed to his leading lady, 'Darling, what has gone wrong with our marriage?' At that moment a large moth flew out of his flies. It's not often that you get signals from heaven to tell you exactly what's missing from your life. Or do you? Unhappiness is a signal that, whatever you're doing, you're not doing what's right for you. So talk about what's right for you and about those feelings inside you.

2 *There are no medals for unhappiness*. Nobody need be unhappy, miserable, beset by conflicting emotions. They can be sorted out, dealt with. With emotions, and dealing with them, there is no failure. There is only wasted time, so why lock yourself in your own emotional prison?

3 *Don't think too much about yourself, try thinking of others*. There is a great deal of suffering in the world and a great deal to be done about it. Self-pity in the face of this enormous suffering is wrong. So *do* something about yourself, so that you can do more for others.

4 *Attend to your body*. Go for a swim or a walk regularly.

Join a keep fit class. Buy a bicycle. Join a gym, or Weight Watchers. The body affects the mind and vice versa. If your body is over-weight and sluggish, you will feel depressed (and have low self-esteem). You pay attention to your car, have it serviced regularly, look after it; so why not do the same with your body? (More about this in Chapter 6.)

5   *Stimulate your mind.* Join a group or evening class. There is a wide variety of subjects you can choose. Why not choose something different, something that leads on to new interests, new ideas (and new friends)? Try antiques, pottery, archaeology, screen printing, tap dancing. The mind needs servicing too if you are to deal in a robust and honest way with your emotions.

6   *Don't deny your emotions.* If you are depressed, *don't* believe it if somebody says, 'It's the weather.' This is what people often say to me when I'm down and I know it's nothing to do with the weather. I have a friend who I meet regularly for a drink. I moan to him for two hours and then he moans to me for two hours — about life. I feel a lot better after those 'get it off your chest' sessions; even when it's pouring down outside.

7   *Accept yourself.* Nobody wants you to be perfect. Nobody would like you if you were. I certainly would have nothing in common with you.

8   *Not too much psychology.* Learn to understand yourself a little more, but be sure to take that vital first step towards others at the same time. Interminable self-analysis will get you nowhere (except put fancy names on those things you know are wrong with you already).

9   *Don't forget the human spirit.* Notice the pain, the cruelty and the suffering in the world, but don't overlook the beauty, and the courage in other people. It is there in the fields, the sea and the sky — and in the hearts of other people. Take a delight in the flowers, and in nature as a whole. There is beauty around us, and it will lift your spirit if you can train yourself to notice it.

10 *Feed your spirit.* Feed it through contact with people who can encourage you and through contact with beauty and truth. An old man once told me a poem, I'm afraid I don't know where it comes from, but I think the words contain an important truth.

If thou of fortune be bereft
And of thine earthly store have left
Two loaves, sell one, and with the dole,
Buy hyacinths, to feed the soul.

Human beings were meant to be happy some of the time. What
happens to us is what we allow to happen.

Chapter 5

Worried Blue Eyes, Cheltenham

May I introduce two friends of mine? First, there is Roy, aged 42, married with two beautiful teenage children. I'm sitting in his garden which has an immaculate lawn and a swimming pool. It is a gorgeous, sunny afternoon and butterflies flutter in and out of the buddleia tree. Roy's house is enormous and he has enough money to be financially secure for the rest of his life. Roy's sitting in a deck-chair and drinking a gin and tonic. 'T,' he says to me, 'I'm worried.' Why? Not enough ice in his drink? Musing over the fact that butterflies have such short lives? Thinking that it might rain tomorrow? 'What are you worried about?' I ask him. He looks at me and adjusts his sun-glasses.

'Life, Tom,' he says, 'life.'

Second, there is Aurelia, aged 34, a single parent with a daughter, aged 11. She lives in a small terraced house. The living room is tiny. On the day I visit her the rain is pitiless and water drips from her ceiling into a bucket in the middle of the carpet. The house is falling to bits: windows broken, dry rot, a large crack in the wall. I find it absolutely unbearable. Outside, a large crack of thunder rends the air and the drips into the bucket become louder and more rapid.

'T,' Aurelia says, 'Do you read Auden? I just adore his poetry.' While she quoted Auden, she absent-mindedly emptied the bucket into the kitchen sink, put it back on its place on the carpet, and sat down on the battered old settee.

'And Philip Larkin, too. Isn't he wonderful?' She offers to make me a cup of tea as she reaches out for a copy of *The Whitsun Weddings*. I look up at the ceiling, in terror.

I mention Roy and Aurelia to illustrate an obvious — but central — point: there's no direct correlation between worry (what's going on *in here*) and our environment (what's going on *out there*). Some people are just worriers. Roy, for instance, having no stresses that I can think of, worries constantly: about his health, his family, his investments, his life. I think that worry has become a habit for him; he just seems to need something to worry about.

What is important in life is not the facts but the interpretation we put upon the facts, not our world but what we make of our world. The world, like the weather, just *is*. It's our reactions to it that make us happy or miserable, able to cope or riddled with anxiety.

Some people, like Aurelia, live in surroundings that would frighten hell out of the most hardened individuals, yet they exude an air of tranquillity, of *coping*. How do they do it? Why aren't people such as Aurelia reduced to neurosis, paralysis, breakdown? Why aren't they filled with a daily sense of foreboding and *Angst*? Can we learn anything from these non-worriers?

Yes and no. Worry is fear spread thin, a sense of danger or threat. It's that feeling of the jitters, or the feeling that something nasty is about to happen. Some people experience it every day; for some of us worry is a constant companion; even when everything's fine.

I once had a student who was a very highly strung young man, what my mother used to call 'a bag of nerves'. He came to see me one morning, saying, 'Something's very wrong. The flat's great, I'm on good terms with the bank manager and my love-life's fine. I'm very worried.' I asked him whether he'd done the piece of work I'd set him a month previously. 'Oh, hell, no,' he said. 'Oh, thanks a lot,' he added. Worry for him wasn't so much an old friend as a Siamese twin. He needed to worry, so I gave him what he needed: something *specific* to worry about. But it wasn't just that. Now he also had a plan of action, something to do. It is always better, in my view, to do something, anything, rather than to just sit there worrying. Worry really can make our lives a living hell. The sad thing is that it never solved anything.

One of the main difficulties with worry is that the feeling of foreboding is there but often one isn't sure where the danger is coming from; the nagging doubts and jitters become chronic simply because one cannot pinpoint the danger; worry then becomes a habit and we start to worry about trivial things as well as things that really matter.

59

With people who do worry you can't say, 'Don't worry.' They do and that advice will make them worry more. What you have to do is to come up with a programme of action: give them something to do that will increase their self-confidence. You have to reduce their anxiety so that they can use it as a stimulus to awareness, and as a trigger to getting something done about their situation and themselves. Coping is learning to live within limitations — one's own, and one's situation. We have to see each day as an opportunity for growth. We have to see life as a series of challenges, of problems to be tackled, rather than a never-ending vista of impending disasters.

Let's have a look at some of the things that people worry about, are obsessed with: things that make them say, 'I can't cope.' How do we give such people confidence and self-esteem and give them the encouragement to cope, and to move on from coping to really enjoying their lives? Worry can be extremely debilitating: it can ruin our happiness. So what do we do about it?

The people who write to my 'On The Couch' column in *Cosmopolitan* worry about all sorts of things: the world, their relationships with others, their emotions, their relationship with a special other, their lack of confidence, their low self-esteem, their figures, their weight, their families/lovers/friends. To many of them the problem that they have seems insoluble: they have come to a closed door in their lives, can't seem to open it; they've reached a 'Y' junction and cannot decide which way to go.

I receive hundreds and hundreds of letters and I find it sad that so many people do write to me. Agony aunts and uncles are the priests of modern society, people to whom many thousands of people make confession by post. It seems as though a great many people have nobody to share their problem with, *nobody to talk to*, nobody to whom they can reveal their deepest worries and fears. Of those who write to me, 95 per cent are women, which may reflect the fact that men, who do have conflicts and worries, are conditioned by society not to be open about their feelings, not to discuss what is going on inside them, even with an agony uncle at a safe distance. This is one of the saddest points of all.

My job is quite simple. I provide encouragement. I also outline the choices open to my correspondent as I see them. I try to give them the courage to take the step(s) that will solve the problem. The philosophy is one of *action*. Thought, and advice, is rehearsal for the deed. Rehearsal is a waste of time if the drama − that opening of the closed door − never takes place. In my book, words score 0; deeds score 10.

Let's have a look at some people's worries, and the solutions that I suggest. You may disagree with some of them. In that case, you could try your hand at thinking what your answer would have been.

'I am 17,' S writes, 'and I find it increasingly difficult to work out the meaning of the world I have (involuntarily) been thrown into. At 16 I left school after passing only one exam and got a job in a local factory. I know how lucky I am but I can't help moaning and feeling trapped. I don't know how people can work in this sort of place for ever. It may sound silly but I feel under a lot of pressure. I find it hard to do anything but eat compulsively or watch TV. The slightest suggestion from my mum about anything sparks off World War III. It's not my mum that's doing wrong but it's not me either. I seem to be taking everything out on her: blaming her for my freckles and for my being overweight.

I don't know any other way to release my built-up anxiety and frustration than to cry when I'm on my own. It's a private depression that I know many other people have.

The first thing you need to answer this letter effectively is sympathy: you have to care about the person. If you don't care, it will show through in your reply. The second thing you need is empathy: you have to imagine what it's like to be in her shoes, in her situation. It's not pleasant. It's like being trapped in a lift. It's like being lost on a dark night and not sure of which road to take. It's awful.

I once saw an experiment with a rat. The rat was placed on a stand and forced, by a sudden release of a blast of hot air behind it; to jump to either a white card or a black card. If he jumped to white, he was rewarded with cheese; if he jumped to black he fell down from that stand into a wire net, which was painful. Then, the really nasty bit happened. The white card became darker; the black card became lighter. They soon became the same shade of grey. The rat didn't know what to do, where to jump. He ended up running in circles around the laboratory floor, squeaking loudly, totally neurotic. I think even rats deserve better treatment than this. The experiment illustrates, however, how dreadful it feels to be faced with a problem to which there seems to be no solution.

Having sympathized and empathized with S, what advice do we give her? I suggested a simple six-point plan of action to get her moving, to get her living her life rather than sitting there, terribly frustrated, crying in solitude. You may or may not agree with the points I make.

- *Stop blaming mother.* We're all tempted to take part in the blame game, but it is a total waste of time. Leave your mother alone and concentrate on you instead.
- *Do something about those educational qualifications.* Find out what courses are available in the local college and sign on; work towards better exam results – and a job that'll get you out of that factory. Your school stamped you 'failure'. Show them that they're wrong.
- *Stop watching TV.* Join a group, or a class, where you come into contact with people who will encourage you towards something better. Watching the Idiot's Lantern every evening will make you even more depressed than you are already and will confirm your view that the world is a horrible, violent place. It isn't. The world is what we make of it.
- *Get angry.* Say, 'Enough's enough. I'm worth better than this.' Believe that passionately and get involved with people who give you hope. Stop thinking of yourself as a failure. Sitting there, watching TV, you're not using your abilities. No wonder you're frustrated and depressed. Depression is anger turned inwards to get angry about the world, get off your bottom and stop moaning.
- *Believe in something.* Join CND, join a political party, join Save the Whale – join anything, but believe. Believe that you *can* change the world, that you *can* change yourself and that you *can* make the world a better place for you, your mum and all of us.
- *Don't aim for perfection.* Set realistic goals and go for them. To compare ourselves with those who seem perfect can be very demoralizing, so do something about your weight. Eat less, go on a diet. Do it for you, because you want to be fit and the best possible person you can be: not because you want to look like a film star. Lose weight and

start now: you'll feel better for it. Don't imitate others, just get in there and say, 'I'm going to be the best ME I can.' You're not going to be the best you if you're feeling fat and unfulfilled.

Of course, what counts in answering 'On the Couch' letters is the *tone* of the reply. In answering S, my reply in the magazine wasn't quite as blunt as it sounds here. What has to come through more than anything else is that you actually care about what happens to S. If you don't care, you can be the cleverest agony uncle/aunt in the world but your lack of concern will show through. What people need is heart as well as head; encouragement and friendship as well as options.

Let's move from the macro to the micro, to those little things which can damage a friendship between two intelligent, sensible people. It's not always the big issues which can scar a marriage or a friendship: those little nagging issues can do a great deal of damage too. (Look on the box of a game of Trivial Pursuit; you'll find printed there a quotation from Alexander Pope, which reads: 'What mighty contests rise from trivial things.') Let's look at an example.

My husband is a caring, loving and involved father. But he's a perfectionist, while I'm a bumbling head-in-the-clouds idealist. Lately he's started to comment on my accent, my dress and how I never put the keys back on the correct hook. This hurts me. To me, these things are me, just like the nose on my face. I sometimes feel that the essence of me is being destroyed bit by bit. I have phases where I try to change. I try not to interpret every comment as a personal attack but it always slides back into a full-blown confrontation. I'd really like to do something positive, but what?'

When a friend of mine read this letter in *Cosmopolitan* she commented, 'Well, at least her husband *cares*. He wants to improve her; that's better than trading her in for another model.' I wasn't sure about that — it made her sound like a car. Do I give the one I've got a complete re-spray or buy another one?

Another friend said to me, after the letter had been published (nobody, except me, reads the letters to 'On The Couch', they're confidential), 'He's married a flute and he's trying to change her

63

into a violin — absolutely senseless.' My own view was that X wants to save her marriage, so this is what I advised:

- *Stop playing games.* Stop acting the naughty child and letting him take the role of stern father. Treat each other as adults.
- *Seek help from the human resources available.* Go along to the local Marriage Guidance Council and discuss the problem with a trained, neutral person.
- *Grow up.* Say to her husband, 'I love you and I want this marriage to work.' Make an effort to stop doing those things which annoy him (eg, write on the back of her hand in indelible ink: *Key on hook*). Marriage, like any other relationship, is a trade-off. Each partner has to give as well as take.
- *Tell him to stop his nagging.* Point out that they're in a marriage not in a play called *Pygmalion* with him as Professor Higgins and her as Eliza Doolittle. Tell him that conditional love (I'd love you if you didn't wear jeans) isn't as good as gift love (I give my love willingly to you, as you are, without conditions, as a gift from me to you).
- *Work out what she wants from her marriage.* Then, tell him, quietly and without fuss.
- *Say hello to him, as husband, the father of her child and a friend.* With a bit of commitment, common sense and love this can all be solved. 'Stop treating me as a child,' she must tell her husband. Then, she must grow up herself. It takes two to tango, two to make a marriage work.

I get thousands of letters about people's feelings, their inner world. Those feelings range from grief, darkest despair to ecstasy and joy. (People, I'm glad to say, write to me when they're very happy as well as when they're very sad.) I get letters about jealousy, rage, anger, fear, despair, lack of confidence, loss, abandonment, shame, guilt: the whole range of human emotions. What do we do with those feelings? Are there any general principles that may help people who are stricken with grief, consumed with anger or jealousy, or obsessed with the feeling that they aren't worth very much? These kinds of emotions are very painful indeed. What can we do about them? Some of the following might help:

- *Know you're entitled.* You are entitled to worry, feel bad, feel despair. You are entitled to feel as you do. It is not a sin. If you *must* grieve, or worry, or cry, go ahead and cry. You are entitled to those feelings you have, they're real.
- *Share your emotions.* Acknowledge them, hold them up to the light, tell other people about them. They'll understand more about those dark places of the heart than you think. Some of us have been there too.
- *Get help if you need it.* There are many organizations who will help (see the Appendix) and *will* understand your problem. Don't try to go it alone if it means that, going alone, you are heading towards despair. Others understand. They will help.
- *Acknowledge the pain.* First comes the past, then the pain as we re-live the past, then the guilt (as we blame ourselves for what happened), then the choice. The choice is, do we face up to the pain and move on or do we live in the past? It's as simple as that.
- *Having nothing to do with guilt.* It's a stupid, crippling emotion. It *wasn't* your fault. Others were there too. Forgive those others, forgive yourself, and move on.
- *Be good to yourself.* You have a right to those feelings. You have as much right to walk this earth as any of us. You belong here just as much as the birds and the trees. Don't apologize for your own existence. You don't have to do that. You're entitled to be alive, so walk on, hold your head up high and say, 'I have as much right to be here on this beautiful earth as anyone else. I don't have to apologize to *anybody* for being me.'

Two recurrent themes in letters to 'On The Couch' are self-doubt and lack of confidence. Many of the women who write to me suffer from low self-esteem. Consider the following letter. It's about a relationship with a special other. It's also about depression and low self-regard.

My boyfriend and I have been seeing each other for about a year and I'm not sure whether to continue the relationship. I'm scared of ending it in case I make a great mistake; also, because I've suffered so much depression and confusion for the last six years of my life (pills, psychiatrists, group therapy for months) that I'm frightened I'll become depressed again.

65

He says he loves me very much and it's an accepted fact by all who know us that the relationship will be a permanent one. I believe he loves me; I believe he is genuinely ignorant to my needs. I have faith in him to make something of his career and all these reasons make me hold on to our relationship. I love him.

Yet I'm growing tired of almost playing mummy to him, of being the strong one, of reassuring him. Perhaps he'd be better off with somebody who accepts his chauvinistic ways and attitudes. I'm very attractive; people find me friendly and outgoing (I hide my sadness excellently). At the moment I wish I had someone strong to lean on, someone who'd spoil me a bit and take the initiative. Please advise me as the seeds of depression are beginning to sprout and grow again, and this harvest may be one too many.

What would you say to this young woman? I suspect that her life motto is: this will all end in tears. Some people *do* assume that no good will come from any enterprise that they undertake. Others take the line that everything will turn out fine and, if it doesn't, too bad. Sometimes (always?) what happens to us is what we allow to happen. With ourselves, as with other people, attitude is all. My advice to this lady was as follows:

- *It isn't an opinion poll.* Do what's right for you, what works for you. What does it matter what your friends — or your Aunt Maud — thinks?
- *In your assessment of the relationship, go for the 70 per cent solution.* He's ignorant of your needs — why not tell him, quietly, what they are? — but you love him. Only you can say whether your love means more to you than that percentage of his behaviour that gets on your nerves.
- If you're tired of being mother, stop. Tell him that it's his turn to be the strong one, and tell him to cut out the chauvinism. Take turns at being strong.
- *Forget about a strong man to lean on.* When we give the whole of the responsibility for ourselves to another person it is, in the long run, a disabling rather than an enabling experience. Take charge of your own life and say, 'I'm worth the best and I intend to get it.'
- *Give up the doom-laden philosophy.* Nothing is inevitable. Deciding is what life is about. Do you want this man or

66

don't you? You love him (and he loves you), so work on him and make it clear what you want: *quality*. If he isn't up to it, drop him. Know *why* you're doing what you do: because you're an OK person, and things will turn out fine, with him or without him. So learn to believe in *yourself* and stop canvassing your friends about every decision you make.

What lies behind *all* the answers given to those who write to 'On The Couch' is a philosophy. It consists of three major beliefs: (a) we have choice and we *can* change ourselves, and the situation we're in, if we really want; (b) to make that change often takes courage; my job, as an agony uncle, is to provide options and en-*couragement*; (c) we write the scripts of our own lives and our lives remain unfulfilled if we constantly ask others to write our life-scripts for us.

Consider the following letter. It gives, I think, encouragement to the rest of us, holds out that possibility of change, emphasizes the necessity of positive action and illustrates how that closed door in our life can be opened. Not all the letters I receive are dismal. This one cheered me up and made my day. People really can get out of that dark tunnel of worry, negative thoughts and destructive emotions if they have the courage to take that first step.

For several years I was mixed up, often feeling low and lonely, cutting myself off from other people. This time last year I was in a very bad way. I was a compulsive eater and hated myself: enough to try to end the lifeless existence I led.

My doctor referred me to group therapy and I went every week to talk and listen and learn about myself. Suddenly, round about Easter, the sun shone: I felt completely different. One day I suddenly knew that I was an OK person – no saint, but able to hold my own and give myself a chance. I started to smile more, to wear brighter clothes, to go on a diet. I liked myself!

Last summer I applied for, and got, a job abroad. I could make the move because I had the support of my friends and family and I knew I wouldn't lose it by moving further away. I miss them all, of course, but the good thing is knowing that I made the decision; I have the control over my life and I'm using it.

I don't know why I suddenly changed: I suspect it was a

gradual process inside. I think learning to know myself in group therapy helped but I also find that my new philosophy of life — to live every day as fully as possible and share it with others — is a terrific help to me.

This shows what can happen if you can find a little courage, be just a little bit kinder to yourself, dare to take the first step towards 'something better'. Really, it's about gaining confidence, step by step, so we *do* believe in ourselves, and in the fact that there are lots of marvellous people in this world, we should give ourselves a chance to meet them.

We began with Roy, a very rich man, in his beautiful garden, worrying. What would I say to him about worry? I wouldn't tell him to count his blessings; I wouldn't tell him about the awful things that happen to people who write to me at *Cosmopolitan*; I don't think that would have any effect on him at all. I might say, 'Worry if you want to, you're entitled, but if you want your children to grow up courageous, optimistic and true to themselves, it wouldn't be a bad idea to be that sort of person yourself.'

Then I might read him a poem sent to me by a reader. It's an Ancient Sanskrit poem and I think it is very beautiful:

> Look to this day
> for it is life
> the very life of life.
> In its brief course lie all
> the realities and truths of existence
> the joy of growth
> the splendour of action
> the glory of power.
> For yesterday is only a memory
> and tomorrow is only a vision
> but today well lived
> makes every yesterday
> a memory of happiness
> and every tomorrow a vision of hope.
> Look well, therefore, to this day.

A reader wrote this morning to 'On The Couch'. 'How do I stop worrying?' she asked. 'I worry all of the time, about everything.'

68

'To stop worrying,' I told her, 'you have to *believe* in something: something worthwhile.' Then I told her one or two others things, but — by now — you'll probably be able to guess what I said.

This is not just theory. I live it myself. I've learned not to worry about tomorrow and I don't care what happened yesterday. I've learned that, if you extract all you can each day, you'll have as happy a life as you're meant to have. There *are* days when I press the panic button, but that's a spur to action. The simple rule is: it is always better to *do something* than worry. Worry is rust upon the soul, and my advice is: have nothing to do with it. It really doesn't solve a thing.

Chapter 6
More thoughts on the 'body beautiful'

Time: last summer. *Place*: Weymouth beach. I sit in a deckchair, eating an ice-cream and (in the cause of science) take a good look at some of the holidaymakers lying on the sand or walking along the promenade. Most of these people are, body-wise, less than ideal. They come in all shapes and sizes: tall/short/fat/thin/lightly suntanned/boiled red, like lobsters. None of them look as though they've stepped from the pages of a fashion magazine; none look like people in *Dallas* or *Dynasty*. Some of them look like those bags of sweets they sell off cheaply under the name 'Mis-shapes'.

It isn't only me who has noticed how different from a Greek statue most of us look. A friend of L. S. Lowry once asked him why he painted people of such peculiar shapes. 'Let's go for a walk,' said Lowry. The two went for a stroll around the streets of Salford and there they all were, those people in the paintings: thin, stooped over, large feet, large heads. Most people, if you think about it, are less than ideally proportioned. Women who watch beauty contests – and who listen to the contestants' bust/waist/hip measurements being read out – do so in a spirit of wonder (and envy?) rather than in the hope of saying, 'Fancy that. Just the same as me.'

To avoid any charges of sexism, let me say that I, too, own a body which is less than ideal (as do many men). I am, at least, a stone overweight. I have pitifully thin arms, like pipe cleaners. Sitting down, I look normal. Standing up, you notice that I have the body of a man of 6′ 2″ placed, fairly and very squarely (with my stomach sticking out), on ridiculously short legs. Very seldom in films or on TV does the hero look like me. The hero is usually tall, with a full head of hair. I look more like the villain, or the one who *never* gets the girl.

How do I cope with this distressing fact? I've learned to live with it. I've got used to buying clothes and seeing Oliver Hardy staring back at me from that long mirror. I used to worry dreadfully about my body when I was a teenager. Now, I tell people that, when I was a teenager, I was 6' and had blue eyes. It's just that the worries of the world have made me shrink, and my eyes change colour. One woman, in a mixed sauna, said to me, 'I've seen better bodies.' Such a remark would have wounded my pride at one time. I merely asked her, 'Have you seen worse?' She had, so that's fine by me. I must be somewhere in the middle, reasonably ordinary. I'm no movie star.

One fantasy I have is that, if I were 6' 2" and handsome, all my problems would be solved. You probably yearn to lose weight, have a slightly different-shaped face and then the world would be your oyster. It's another ideal fiction. Let's forget about me, you and those people on Weymouth beach, and talk about beautiful people and whether *they* have problems. Surely, as they have what the rest of us want, they don't?

We can argue over whether Chartres Cathedral, garden gnomes or a painting by Vermeer is beautiful. Most of us would agree that there are some people who *are* beautiful. They fall, like Greta Garbo, Clark Gable. Sophia Loren, into a special category and it is interesting to observe the effect that these beautiful people have on the rest of us.

I was at a party last year when I heard a friend of mine, a townie and a person who *loathes* the countryside, talking with enthusiasm to a farmer about his pigs. 'You hypocrite,' I said to her after the party. 'You hate pigs.' She looked at me. 'I know,' she said, 'but he *was* incredibly handsome, wasn't he? Quite godlike. I'd sell my soul for a man like that, never mind tell a few white lies.' Beauty is power. It can enchant and enslave. It can also lead to problems.

Take Paula. I would. Anywhere. 'I wouldn't invite Paula to my party,' women tell me. 'There's something about her I don't like.' I know. No woman wants to see her man reduced to a gibbering idiot, standing by Paula as though he'd just been sandbagged. Paula *is* beautiful. Her beauty doesn't make her popular with women; it only makes her popular with men. That makes Paula's life more isolated than it looks from where you and I are standing. We're in the middle. It can be lonely in that special 'beautiful' category.

I wouldn't like to be beautiful. It would waste so much time.

Checking to see that you still had your looks, that they hadn't disappeared overnight. Worrying about whether your looks will vanish with age (which they sometimes do, sometimes don't, which is why older beautiful people still worry). Wondering whether men or women like you for you or whether they want to be seen with you merely to add to their status and prestige. Being beautiful doesn't solve life's problems: it sets up a whole new set of problems, some of them very tricky indeed. Who would want to be beautiful?

It doesn't mean to say that you (and I) don't want to look attractive, make the best of ourselves. People have always wanted to do that and they always will. When a friend of mine left her husband, after a really magnificent farewell speech, she had to go back an hour later for her moisturizing cream. 'I felt such a fool,' she told me, 'but I'd never go anywhere without *that*.' I'm told that the last words of Charles I, before they chopped his head off, were, 'Is my wig straight?' Even *in extremis* looks count, so it seems.

Why shouldn't you take a pride in yourself? You don't have to be a 10, a raving beauty, to meet someone who will *see* you as a 10 – and beautiful. Your beauty (and mine) is in the eye of a loving beholder. For every pot there is a lid. For ever 7 there's another 7 who will collude in the useful fantasy that both are beautiful to each other. This is what counts. You may be ordinary, but all you need to know is that someone, somewhere, sees you as beautiful.

This is why to dress attractively, use appropriate make-up and to have a healthy body is sound common sense. It keeps the doors of love open to those who want to see you as beautiful. It boosts your ego to receive compliments. You *feel* good when you look good and you (like me) know when you look your best. Making the most of yourself is very sensible indeed. It's being you, *being beautiful in your own way*.

What isn't so sensible is to compare with beautiful women, to strive for some ideal fiction and to despair when you fall short of that impossible mark. For women to compete with Joan Collins, Brooke Shields or Sophia Loren simply isn't sane or necessary. For men to try to be like Robert Redford, Robert de Niro or Paul Newman is daft. It simply means that the magic which is you, the uniqueness which is you, never gets a chance to see the daylight. As you strive for your impossible dream, your ideal fiction, you're missing all the fun that comes from relaxing, being you (and making the most of *you*).

The secret is to be attractive *at your own age and stage* and not compete the whole time with air stewardesses, film stars, TV announcers, TV personalities who are young. To equate beauty with youth is to see life as a ski-run, downhill all the way after the age of 25. There is no greater embarrassment than to see a woman, or man, dressed — and acting like — a person half her/his age.

The issue isn't whether your body is plump or thin, but whether you are being your own person. Autonomy, not anatomy, is the crux of the matter: being yourself and learning to accept your limitations. Long eyelashes, losing that 6 lb, may be important to you but are those things really more important than having fun, relating warmly to people, living your life?

To be beautiful *may* be to be kissed by the gods (although I doubt it). I'd rather be kissed by X, a lady I met recently, who made my tiny heart go pit-a-pat and whom you wouldn't pick out as being particularly beautiful. This is the advantage the rest of us have over those people who *are* beautiful: we have much more fun making other people wonder what we can possibly see in each other.

On the subject of beauty, I think you should remember the following rules, which will help you to enhance, rather than lower, your self-esteem:

● *Be fit, clean and well turned out, but don't get obsessed with your large behind/thin legs.* Remember, other people are far too worried about theirs to notice yours.

● *If you're dumpy, be magically dumpy.* Highlight your good points. Don't pretend to be a pencil if you're meant to be a golf ball; just be the most attractive plump lady on the block.

● *Don't model yourself on Farrah Fawcett/Clint Eastwood.* Why should you? Experiment with your looks and come up with the Best You. That's always better than a poor version of that Impossible Dream.

● *Not all beautiful people are happy.* What counts in life is not what we've been given in the way of looks, but how we use the looks we've been given.

● *Lots of ordinary people have plenty of friends (and a very happy sex life).* Relationships between people depend on warmth and openness and not on hair styles and high cheekbones. Sexual bliss doesn't depend on being beautiful. If it did, most of us would be celibate.

● *Real beauty is more than fashion*. It is a combination of body and mind and has a subjective element. It is because we're so obsessed with rating scales that we get so depressed about it (ie, 'How do I rate compared with Anna Ford/Roger Moore?' Why bother to ask?). If you believe yourself to be attractive, you will be. Other people tend to accept the way in which you see yourself. See yourself as dowdy and uninteresting and they'll see you that way too. See yourself as no oil painting, but interesting and attractive and others will concur in your judgement.

Every human being has a *self-image*, a way in which he/she perceives himself/herself. You have a name, a gender, social class, a job (if you have a job), interests, hobbies and a body image (what *you* think your body looks like). Everybody has an *ego-ideal* (ie, the sort of person you would like to be). There will inevitably be a gap between your self-image and your ego-ideal (since human beings are always moving towards some goal, always *becoming*). The size of that gap may determine your level of *self-esteem*. It all depends how realistic, how attainable your dreams and aspirations are. Happiness may be the difference between what we have and what we want.

Let's think about this in terms of beauty. You are, say, fairly plain so you work on yourself, watch your weight, use suitable make-up, wear clothes that suit you. You keep yourself reasonably fit. Fit for what? Fit enough to enjoy life, to live your existence to the full, to feel good. (Not fit enough to run in a marathon, but fit enough to run for a bus and to play tennis, or any other game you want to play.) You are not in a competition with X, who plays squash every day and is super fit. You are fit because you want your body, as well as your mind, to be alive, responsive, well. You aim to achieve your ego-ideal, you at your best.

Now consider people who have very high (or fantasy) ego-ideals. I have a friend who is not beautiful but who is *extremely* attractive. She is always worried about her appearance: her looks, her weight, her figure, her wrinkles (she hasn't any), her need to lose 6 lb in weight. (She has no need to lose 6 lb in weight; recently she's looked positively thin; I reckon she needs to put a stone *on*.) I, and all her other friends, tell her she looks attractive but all she says is, 'I know I look awful.' Who is she competing against? Could it be one of those women in *Dallas* or

Dynasty? Could it be perfection? If it is she's on to a loser. Perfection is too far away from any of us to reach it. Why not learn to live with your imperfections rather than strive for a goal that (a) will never be reached and (b) the pursuit of which provides no enjoyment?

Aiming for an ego-ideal that is within reach is the key. This explains why very plain, or ugly, people can have high esteem. It explains why X, at the office, is such a hit with men despite having a face that one would think only a mother could love and a figure like a punctured water bed. X has personality, spark, zest for life, and a great sense of humour (and sense of fun), She's not self-conscious; she's not obsessed with her looks (or her figure). Sure, she'd like to lose a couple of stone, but she doesn't let it affect her life too much. She has the knack of speaking to everyone as though that particular person was her best friend. She listens to people: she's warm, friendly, genuinely interested in others. At the moment she's dating the best-looking man in the office. I wonder why?

Ego-ideals are for the picking. We choose our ego-ideals and I'm sure that, in these days of women's striving for equality with men, more and more women will model themselves less on film stars or TV stars with beautiful bodies, but on women in public life whose minds and personalities they admire. There's more to attractiveness than the face, or the body. Personality is vitally important.

In his *Republic*, Plato tells a parable about men and women living in a cave. The inmates have their legs and necks in irons, cannot move and can only see what is in front of them, flickering on the wall, on the other side of the fire. What they see on the wall are shadows cast by the fire on to the side of the cave opposite them. The people take these shadows to be real life, the shapes to be real people, the flickering images to be the real world. They don't know that there is a world, the real, wide, wonderful world outside.

I'm often reminded of Plato's parable of the cave when I watch television. All those flickering figures, ghosts, shadows, from *Dallas*, *Dynasty*, *Starsky and Hutch*, *Miami Vice* and *Cagney and Lacey*. Those people aren't real. They're part of a world of flickering shadows. Yet, real or not, it is surprising how many people model themselves on TV stars (and/or film stars). It's a dangerous business. It's as well to be careful in picking an ego-ideal. Why model yourself on a household name when you

75

have your very own name? Why try to be like someone else, only to be dispirited when you notice the gap that still exists between you and your ego-ideal? If you had real confidence in yourself it would be a source of mystery why Victoria Principal — or one of those Ewing men — wasn't striving desperately to look a little more like you.

Why reach out to the world in a frenzy of worry and self-consciousness about your face/body? It's your face. If your body worries you, do something about it. All that anxiety makes it much harder for people to reach out to you. Why have a great iron ball of self-doubt strapped to one ankle when you could be dancing to the beat of your own heart? Those ideal fictions, those shadows, we carry about in our minds do a tremendous amount of harm.

Consider anorexics. Why have they a distorted body image? Why, when they look in a mirror, do they see themselves as fat, gross, disgustingly overweight when you and I can see that they are painfully, and often dangerously, thin? It isn't because they weren't loved as children. It isn't because they aren't loved now. It is to do with love but love of oneself — learning to be kind to oneself, learning to accept love even though we are, all of us, imperfect. Anorexics suffer from pursuit of a shadow, the perfect figure. Since no such figure exists, they set themselves a programme to become thinner and thinner (to be thin = to be loved). Yet it is a fictitious goal, an untruth, an ideal myth. It is a myth that can bring unhappiness, grief and, in some cases, death.

A typical anorexic is conscientious, intelligent, talkative, conventional, likeable. She (most anorexics are female) is also a perfectionist. *Invariably, she lacks self-esteem*. The anorexic is situated at the extreme end of the 'I must look attractive' continuum. For the anorexic there is no 'I'm good enough as I am'. Everything is seen in terms of good and bad, white and black, perfection or failure. To be thin is to be white, good, perfect. To lose weight is to head towards that impossible dream: perfection.

Anorexia is notoriously difficult to treat. Once it gains a hold the illness gains a momentum of its own: the body, starved, begins to feed on itself. The anorexic becomes more and more nauseated at the thought of eating, putting on weight, moving away from that standard of acceptance of her own body which she has set herself. The best cure is prevention: for parents (and

76

GPs) to look out for those signs of fanaticism, perfectionism, faddiness over food, the need to have total control over their eating habits, and their bodies. Anorexia gives its sufferers a feeling that they *are* in control: of their lives, of their bodies, of their hopes and desires. The control is part of that desperate search for perfection.

Anorexia, like bulimia nervosa, is the result of low self-esteem, a distorted body-image and an impossible ego-ideal. Both are not a desire to look better: they spring from a desire to look the best, perfect, unreproachable. To the bulimic, as to the anorexic, food has no associations with love, hospitality, friendship. It becomes the arch enemy in the bulimic's search for that unobtainable standard, that perfectionist dream. To be thin is to be loved and to be the thinnest is to be loved most. Food becomes disgusting, dirty, shameful. To eat is to lose control, to lose ground in the race towards the impossible dream. To fast, to make oneself sick and regurgitate that evil food, is to regain control over one's mind – and body.

Bulimics will go to enormous trouble to hide their illness from others. They will find places to be sick, to regurgitate their food, wherever they are and whoever they are with. They have become obsessed with being loved, with being acceptable to themselves, with being 'ideal'. That ideal moves further away from them as they strive, ever more desperately, to reach it.

Anorexics and bulimics are martyrs. They achieve recognition and attention, in Adlerian terms, by striving to be best (ie, thinnest), to be superior (thinner than you or me), to be a star (sometimes the price of stardom can be very high indeed). They don't understand that none of us are ordinary, that we're all special and that we emphasize and develop our uniqueness better when we co-operate with others rather than compete. To strive to be ideal is to strive on a ladder that reaches up to a floor called loneliness and despair. To strive to be yourself – the best you – in a group, with others, having fun whilst you're doing it is a very different matter.

By counselling – and firm warnings as to the consequences of their actions – bulimics and anorexics can be deterred from their goal of 'perfection'. This counselling is most effective when the condition is spotted in its early stages. As time goes on it becomes more difficult to counsel because of the distorted body image. For an anorexic, or a bulimic, the cry on looking into the mirror is, 'I'm so fat.' That cry can emerge when the body has started to live off its own muscle and the disease has progressed to a dangerous stage.

How sad that young people should follow this dangerous road to self-esteem. What the anorexic is saying is, 'I'm a genius. I'm a star. Mirror, mirror, on the wall, who is the thinnest of us all? I am.' When you're a genius you don't need to be sociable, friendly, courteous, kind, appreciative, *ordinary*. You follow your own road. You can be ill-mannered, obsessed, rude. It's Adler's inferiority complex again. Not happy at being 'good enough', feeling that you are not worth much, you don't settle for being worth something, you only settle for being best. Your body is your fortune and thinnest is the pot of gold. It's the exaggerated form of a message you and I receive every day from the media: thin is good, fat is bad.

This would not be a problem if it referred to health, the dangers of overweight, but it doesn't. It refers to image. The image that you are urged to emulate is that of a slender, lovely film star, the willowy TV personality, the magazine model with her ravishing dress clinging to her skeletal form. This is nothing to do with health. This is vanity. Health is nothing to do with taking an obsessional interest in being 'perfect'. Health is looking after your body so that you can live your life to the full. Health is being well enough to bite the apple of life to the core. It is to do with being able to run for the No. 62 bus, not with creating a new record in the Olympic 100 metres sprint.

Health is to do with the environment. It is to do with polluting fumes that emanate from factory chimneys and car exhausts, with nuclear waste that is dumped into the sea, with the noise of traffic and with the houses we live in. It is to do with adequate health care, for the poor as well as the rich, and with education for health. Health is also to do with personal values, with a positive, meaningful life-style. Lastly, health is to do with the human spirit, with body, mind and soul, working together as a unity, as a *whole* being.

As Fritjof Capra says in his book *The Turning Point* (Flamingo): 'The shift to the value system that the holistic health movement . . . and the ecology movement advocate is further supported by a number of spiritual movements that re-emphasize the quest for meaning and the spiritual dimension of life.' Life, for many people, is a detective story without a plot, a game without any meaning, a journey without any destination. How can a human being be truly healthy if he or she finds life meaningless?

78

I read in the paper this week that 11 per cent of people attend church regularly, although 79 per cent of people said that they believed in God. Those figures are, to me, significant. There are, in the population, 4 per cent 'don't knows' and 17 per cent disbelievers. Of those that believe in God, only a small fraction attend church regularly. This means that there is a large proportion of the population (68 per cent) who have a host of spiritual yearnings waiting for a home, who cannot turn to the church to give expression to the spiritual side of their being. The myth of Christianity, and the rituals of the church, no longer satisfy their spiritual needs.

This, in my view, is why the myths of 'beauty', 'slimness', 'the perfect face and figure' and many of the modern ideal myths have such a powerful hold on us. To chase such phantoms is to chase the air, to increase stress rather than to alleviate it. To escape from the lack of meaning in our lives many of us turn to instant solace, to alcohol, cigarettes, overeating. We escape into the world of television. None of this meets the need for *meaning*. It is moving towards a fragmented rather than holistic concept of human beings – people who can only be kept going by constant drugs, immediate gratification, escape into a dream world.

Britain has the highest death rate from heart disease in Europe. Once Britons reach 45, their life expectancy is amongst the worst in the developed world. Deaths from drugs (including alcohol) are rising. Cigarettes kill 100,000 British people every year. AIDS continues to grow amongst the population. These are all symptoms of a spiritual alienation, a loss of meaning in a world in which the message is: 'Succeed. Succeed. Be the best.' Succeed at what? Be the best at what? Fame is the spur. By its nature it can only be proffered to a small number of people. Those who achieve fame and success have no guarantee of finding happiness, peace of mind. Those who are not famous/household names/beautiful/rich feel failures. They turn to drugs, or promiscuity, to find comfort, they watch erotica or violence on videos; they watch hours of TV which makes their world even more meaningless and fragmented. Health is to do with body, mind and spirit. Where the mind is sick, and the spirit is parched, the body cannot be healthy.

Consider the following case histories:

Case 1. On and on through snow and ice. Michael is 42, a

highly paid executive in an internationally known company. His work involves a great deal of travelling. He has a wife and two children. He sees as much of them as he can but, as he himself has told them, 'My work must come first.'

Michael, feeling ill, goes to see his doctor. He describes his symptoms and is sent to the hospital to have various tests. It transpires that he has a duodenal ulcer. His doctor warns him that his life-style is far too hectic and stressful and that, if he wants to regain his health, he must cut down on his work, stick to a sensible diet, see more of his family and lead a less stressful existence.

Michael ignores all this advice. He has an operation for his ulcer and continues his work pattern exactly the same as before. The result — Michael's health is such that he has had to give up his job and he is now a permanently sick man. If you talk to Michael he says, 'I miss my job terribly. If I could regain my health I'd go back tomorrow. I miss the conferences, my colleagues, visiting other countries, decision-making. Sometimes, I'd stay in my office until 8 pm, making sure everything was all right for a meeting the next day . . .' All Michael's talk is of work. He doesn't mention his family once.

This is work as a drug, as an escape from that very important question, 'What is life about?' To look at Michael is to see a broken man — a man who has lost his physical strength and one who has no spiritual resources to fall back on. Michael was a 'successful' man. He now sees himself as a failure, not somebody who has let himself and his family down but, and still the myth of 'success' persists, somebody who has let down the company.

Case 2. One day my prince will come. Joan is 25, unmarried and works in a large department store. She is *5 stone* overweight. 'I've tried everything,' says Joan. 'You name it — Weight Watchers, keep-fit classes, diets, health farms — nothing seems to work.' As Joan is talking, she is munching a chocolate which she has just taken out of a large box. She is sitting in an armchair. I would guess that her weight is roughly 13 stone. Her complexion is pallid. Her movements are slow and laboured. She looks far from healthy.

What strikes me, as I listen to Joan, is how small and circumscribed her world is. She never once mentions other people. She talks about her job, her attempts to lose weight, her unfortunate experiences with men. 'I've given up with men,' she says. She doesn't mention politics, the Third World, the neighbours, the Bomb, current issues in the newspapers. She is totally bound up with herself. 'I used to be quite slim at one time,' she tells me. 'I seem to have lost heart recently.' I found that a striking phrase. This seemed to me to be a basically nice person, but living a life which had no purpose, no aim, no meaning other than a narcissistic pursuit of a slim figure.

'There may be good men around,' says Joan.'Maybe I've been unlucky. Maybe one day my prince will come.' She reaches for another chocolate. There is very little self-esteem. How can there be when the over-riding purpose of one's whole life is to lose 6 lb (or, as in Joan's case, 5 stone)? It is the barrenness of Joan's existence, especially her inner existence, which causes her weight problem. It is because she believes in so little that she constantly reaches out for the chocolates.

This (you say) is all rather dismal. It is. It's when you and I — all of us — adopt a much more robust and sensible attitude towards the body beautiful that we'll be able to cope much better with life and to have a chance of reaching out towards happiness. To be beautiful is not necessary (and some beautiful people would say not even desirable). To be spiritually, mentally and physically healthy is desirable simply because it lets you live your life in a way that you have a chance of reaching the best things that life can offer.

To be healthy in body and mind you must learn to:

- *Accept yourself more as you are.* This doesn't mean you shouldn't improve yourself to the extent of *your* potential. You can, and should, make the best of your hair, your skin, your looks, your health.
- *Give up, throw in the dust-bin, ideal myths, impossible dreams, unattainable ideals (and role models).* People may suggest what you should look like. They cannot, or should not, *dictate* what you should look like. If you obey these dictats you will end up miserable, because you'll never reach the ideal and you'll become dissatisfied with everything about you rather than working on a sensible course of self-improvement.
- *There is no failure when you have self-esteem.* You just look *your* best, feel *your* best. It's only when you match

81

yourself against some impossible ideal that the notion of 'failure' comes through the door to make your life miserable.

- *Those who live by the mirror become depressed by the mirror.* There is so much more to life than the way you *ought* to look. (And who says you have to look that way?) There is feeling good, enjoying life, enjoying other people, enjoying the beauty of the world.

- *Do it your way.* Use make-up to suit you. Have a hair style that suits you. Exercise in your own way, a way that releases your energy and stretches you. Don't compare yourself with others, exercise wise. Let them do what makes *them* feel good. Never mind 'going for the burn' (or competing with the rest of the class). If you feel better for exercising your way, stick to it.

- *Set realistic goals for yourself when it comes to losing weight (and getting a better figure).* Take small steps; be proud of what you achieve. Join any organization in which you can gain encouragement and support. Don't compete with others. *Do it for you.* It's when you do it for others (or to reach that unattainable ideal) that discouragement and despair set in.

- *Give time to your life, as well as to your looks.* Have some real purpose in your life, something you are actively involved in and really believe in. That will put those spurious, dictated notions of beauty in their place. Beauty is to do with the mind and soul as well as the body.

- *Don't try to be a 10.* Those 10s are very isolated people. It's better to be a 7. There are enough 7s around for somebody else to see you as a 10, as quite beautiful. Beauty isn't something that somebody orders you to be. Beauty is in the eye of a loving beholder. If you have self-esteem, and believe in yourself, you will inspire that love. It's harder to inspire anybody when you're trying to be somebody else all the time.

- *You have rights too. You have a right to walk this earth, you have a right to hold your head up high as you are. You have a right to be you.* Nobody can turn you into a pale shadow of an ideal myth without your consent. Nobody can make you feel insecure about your looks and your body without your consent. Don't give that consent.

- *Never compare.* If anybody tells you that you look like a famous film star or well-known TV personality say, 'Who's she? I'm me. I look like me.' You will only make yourself sad and miserable if you constantly want to look like somebody else.

- *Aim to look better; never aim to look best.* It's the competitive aspects of looks, bodies and health that do so much damage. Set the goal to suit you. Who cares what others are aiming at? The competition is with you. If you are big, be big. Go on a diet if you wish, for your own reasons, but don't ever do it to be slimmer than Mrs Jones down the road. Mrs Jones is enough to make anybody depressed, she's so slim. Mrs Jones is herself depressed. She's competing with Mrs Smith, who's even slimmer. Nobody in this chain of sadness and failure has the courage to say, 'I'm me.'
- *With fashion, now, you don't have to conform.* You can wear a skirt at a length *you* like, wear colours that suit you, wear styles that bring out the best in you. This is the attitude you must have towards the body beautiful. Get your body into a shape that suits you, make the most of your looks, dress attractively to suit you. Having done that you've done all that's necessary. You have done your best, look your best. You accept yourself and that is the best way to get other people to accept you too.

Chapter 7
Friendship

I was chatting to a man on a train, who was a company director and obviously a very successful man. 'You know the most important thing in my life?' he asked me. Then he answered his own question. 'Friendship. My best friend is my wife. I'm a very lucky person.'

There is no doubt that friendship is important to people. It provides them with affirmation, relaxation – with a true friend you can be yourself, you don't have to pretend. A friend is someone who likes you, respects you, cares what happens to you. A friend is someone whose company you enjoy, someone you get in touch with when you have good news, or when you're in trouble. A friendship is a mutual admiration society – a support system – consisting of two people.

In my own life friendship has been just as important as sexual love. Grand passions, those magnificent waterfalls in the less accessible regions of the human heart, have swept on their way. My friendships, on the other hand, have been more tranquil, more peaceful, providing me with a sense of well-being and *belonging*.

It's interesting that the *Oxford English Dictionary* defines a friend as 'one joined to another in intimacy and mutual benevolence independently of sexual or family love'. I would add to this that a spouse, as in the case of the man on the train, can also be a friend. So can a parent, brother, sister or cousin. Blood ties don't preclude friendship. Neither does sexual passion. To have a lover who is also a good friend is possible. To love someone passionately, and to know that person is your friend, is heaven indeed.

By and large, we live in an age-segregated society. For example, in the road where I live there is only one family where there are young children. *All* of the other residents are elderly people whose children have grown up and gone away. In an

84

estate not far from here most of the adults are young (ie, between 20 and 40) bringing up young children. In the town there are several nursing homes for the elderly. We segregate children in schools; we tend to see teenagers — and elderly people — as in a different group to ourselves.

This seems rather sad. When I was a boy I lived in a street in which children, teenagers, adults and the elderly all lived in close proximity. There was contact between young and old: grandfathers, grandmothers, aunts and uncles lived near by. It is possible, these days, for people to have friends who are of a vastly different age (or who are related by blood). Usually, though, friends are not relatives; they are normally of roughly the same age group; they can be of either sex, and of any race or creed. A friend is simply somebody you feel close to.

Distance may or may not play a part in friendship. My eldest daughter (who, as a teenager, was the local unpaid agony aunt for the emotionally stricken teenagers of the neighbourhood) has friends all over the world: in the USSR, Australia, France, the USA, Holland — you name it. Her address book bulges with the names of friends in far-flung places and she keeps in touch with them. 'You have to work at friendship,' she tells me. She certainly does. Phone calls, Christmas cards, letters, intermittent reunions, all keep the friendships going. I tend to be lazy in keeping my friendship alive. She isn't, she *does* work at it, and she has friends who she knew as a child with whom she still keeps in touch.

Time may or may not affect friendship. A friend is someone who appreciates you, has something in common with you. A friend is someone who shares your point of view, perhaps has the same sense of humour as yourself. A friend is someone in whose company you can feel at ease, and just be yourself. However, you may change with time so that you no longer have anything in common. Conversely, your friend may change and somebody you once were very close to may have become — over the years — a stranger.

I find this aspect of friendship fascinating. When I was a teenager I was extremely close to X. There was no wearing of masks between us: we told each other our secret fears, our hopes, plans for the future. I knew what X was thinking without him having to say it. We could sit for an hour in silence without saying anything to each other, perhaps drinking a cup of tea, not feeling uncomfortable, perfectly at ease in each other's

85

company. We went abroad together, shared experiences, ideas. I told him about my love life, my latest passion for Sandra or Pamela. He told me the progress of his affairs of the heart. We were friends, buddies, mates. He was my *best* friend.

I say all this because that friendship, begun at school, lasted until we were both about 26 years old. Then we lost touch with each other and there was a twelve-year gap. A mutual friend put us in touch with each other again and we arranged to meet. I looked forward to that meeting with great excitement. I was going to meet my best pal again after all those years.

The reunion was absolutely disastrous. It was very sad, really. We both desperately tried to restore the old intimacy, that closeness, but it simply wasn't there. As X spoke, told me the details of his life, what he'd been doing, what he hoped to do, it dawned on me that we no longer had anything in common. Worse, I felt uncomfortable in his presence. He had changed. He wasn't the person I'd remembered. It was all a big mistake. As we said goodbye we said we'd meet again but we never did. The truth was that we, once great friends, had both changed out of all recognition. We were strangers to each other and all we had in common was a past that couldn't be resurrected.

This is strange because there are people in my life — and I'm thinking primarily of a couple who used to be our next-door neighbours — who, when I meet them, I take up the intimacy, the closeness, the friendship immediately we start talking. The conversation flows as though we've never been away from each other. With these people time — that great thief — certainly doesn't steal my friends away. The friendship is resumed as though there had been a five-minute interval, even though I may not have seen those friends for two or three years. It's there immediately; that empathy, closeness, openness, humour, *celebration* of each other's individuality. Very odd. Distance has kept us apart; time has flown; yet we are as close, as mutually affirming, as we were in those days when we first knew each other.

What's vital in my own friendship is a feeling of trust and sharing: a friend doesn't take advantage of you, put you down, patronize you. You can be vulnerable with a real friend, tell it how it is, show your feelings. There's no pretence. Friendship is about sharing, seeing the world through the same spectacles. It's about trade-offs: I give you what I am and you do the same; you stroke my ego and I stroke yours. You listen to my troubles and joys and I listen to yours. You take off your mask and I take off mine. With a friend you can tell the truth and that includes emotional truth. A real friend knows how you feel and, with a friend, there's no need to disguise or hide those feelings. It's this affirmation of our emotional world, the secret places of the heart, that I consider to be the most crucial part of friendship.

Networks of support are vital to human beings. To have somebody to talk to is vital during the hard times we all go through. To have a friend to talk to halves our misery. It also doubles our joy. When I go to the cinema my pleasure is increased if I have somebody to go with (and to discuss the film with afterwards). First comes the experience; next comes the discussion of that experience. Both are essential to human beings. Human beings find it hard to live alone: they are social animals.

As for therapy, it takes place wherever people gather together in the name of friendship: in kitchens, over a garden fence, in factories, offices, pubs, at bus stops. 'I've had a terrible day,' you say to someone, perhaps enlarging upon your remarks and getting your feelings out of your system. 'We spent two hours talking about her love life. She talked. I listened.' That's therapy. To talk to someone about a problem is the first step to doing something about it.

Informal therapy consists of talking to friends; formal therapy consists of talking to strangers. In her book *Talking to a Stranger* (Fontana Original) Lindsay Knight details the different kinds of formal therapy that exist, how these therapies work and for whom they are meant. She also says how much the therapies cost and whether they are available on the National Health Service.

Ms Knight's book is a consumer's guide to therapy and she is careful to point out that therapy isn't confined to the mentally ill. It is also for people with ordinary problems and those who have got themselves into an emotional tangle that help from a neutral person, a stranger, would help to resolve. Lindsay Knight describes individual and group therapy, sex therapy, counselling, psychotherapy and psychoanalysis of various types. If one approach doesn't work for you, another one might. The book is a very useful guide to the formal therapy presently available to this country.

What strikes me, as an agony uncle for *Cosmopolitan* who therefore receives thousands of letters every year from people who want to write to a stranger, is that there are a great many lonely people in our society: people who don't have a listening ear, people who have inadequate human networks of support, people who are incredibly lonely. Loneliness is a disease and, in our society, it is a very prevalent one. There are many people all around us who don't talk to anybody, who don't receive sympathy and who feel that nobody understands them. There are people who have no friends at all.

This is very sad as it is not difficult to make friends, providing that we are willing to take the first steps in the journey towards friendship. It is because people don't know what these steps are that they are forced to turn to agony aunts and uncles with their problems (or to turn to counsellors and psychiatrists when their loneliness has become so unbearable that they are no longer able to cope with day-to-day living).

In 1666, in his *Maxims*, La Rochefoucauld wrote: 'A true friend is the most precious of all possessions and the one we take least thought about acquiring.' This may be true, but what if you are out of practice at making friends and simply don't know, or have forgotten, how to go about the business of taking those first, simple steps towards friendship?

The first step in making friends is *the deed*: to go somewhere where people are, to join something. This may sound simple enough but this step can be terrifying for people who are shy, for those who have become used to loneliness or for those who find meeting strangers an ordeal.

This fear of meeting others was brought home to me several years ago. As chairman of a local school Parent Teacher Association I visited parents asking them for items for a jumble sale which was to be held the following Saturday. At one house, I asked a woman − a young, very shy, single-parent mother − if she'd like to help on the Friday evening, putting out the jumble, making tea, talking to the other parents. She solemnly promised me that she'd come along to help. She never turned up. I think she wanted to come but she was overcome by shyness when the time arrived. What I should have done, of course, is gone with my car and fetched her to the school (or asked one of the other parents to call for her). This might have given her the moral support to take that *first step* in joining in social functions which is so vital.

What shy people *can* do is to go to the local reference library and look up the various clubs, associations and classes in their area. There will usually be a wide range of evening classes, anything from Cordon Bleu cookery to Beginner's Italian. There may be a film club, a Ramblers' Association, keep fit classes, mother and toddler groups, playgroups, a gardener's club, a tennis club. Commercially run activities may include swimming clubs, ice-skating, roller-skating, tap-dancing classes. There's usually something to suit every taste.

The deed consists of picking something to suit your own taste and *going along to sign on*, something that, for shy or lonely people, takes an enormous amount of guts. Joining something *isn't* always easy − it does take courage − but it is worth it; it's the only way in which any of us can make new friends and open the door to friendship and to those mutual support systems that are so important to us all.

When you have joined something, when you go along that first evening, you'll feel shy and awkward. The thing to remember is to be yourself. Smile at people and say hello. Tell them your name, ask them theirs. Listen to people. Don't try to be witty, clever or smart. People *will* like you if you have the courage to be yourself.

You may be worried that people won't like you because your nose/bottom/feet are too big, or because you're so shy. If you are shy, admit it (you could even say, 'I'm very shy'). Don't try to cover up your shyness by chattering too much or by being argumentative and bombastic. Try to be natural and relaxed. Don't imagine that, when people know more about you, they won't like you. Those other people have their guilty secrets too. What *will* put them off you is a phoney cleverness, or trying to be perfect. (Who wants perfection in other people? Perfection doesn't exist this side of Paradise.)

If you meet somebody you like and find yourself talking to him or her, remember to smile from time to time, to say something complimentary about the other person and to *listen*. Listening is as vital a part of conversation as talking. Don't take yourself too seriously and talk about the interests of the other person. Ask him/her about himself/herself. You can talk about yourself − and your brilliant career − at a later date.

The main enemies of natural conversation (and of making new friends) are high anxiety and fear of rejection. Anxiety makes us talk too much; it makes us too aware of our spots or our big bottom. The truth is that everybody is much too worried about their own appearance to be overly concerned about yours.

Fear of rejection, in a curious way, invites rejection. This is why it's better to be natural and spontaneous, not to try too hard and to let the conversation – and the relationship – develop at its own pace.

If you like a person you've met once or twice, you could ask him/her to meet for a coffee/go with you to the cinema or the theatre or go ice-skating together. Go somewhere where you'll have fun, where you don't have to talk all the time, where you can relax and enjoy each other's company. It may be better to go window shopping than to invite him/her back to your house for a meal. Maybe the thought of preparing and serving dinner will make you nervous, so why not have a meal out, in an inexpensive place, where you can give your friend full attention rather than worrying whether your soufflé has risen as it should?

Once you have summoned the courage to join something, it provides you with an interest and material for conversations. Joining a gardening club is very different from joining a political party, but both give you something to talk *about*. I once had a long conversation on a train with a miner. He didn't talk about coal but about racing pigeons. He was a fascinating man who knew his subject. There were no awkward pauses in the conversation and I was impressed how enthusiastic – and knowledgeable – that man was about his subject. His enthusiasm was catching. This is why it is essential for shy people to join a group of some sort. There they can learn, gain experience. Experience precedes conversation. To converse well you have to have something that absorbs and interests you and something that you believe in.

Friendship involves effort. Virginia Woolf once wrote of the friends she'd lost because she couldn't be bothered to cross the street. Voltaire, on the other hand, tells us that we must always cultivate our garden and our friends. Those people I know with a large number of friends have one thing in common: they all care about their friendships and are willing to take the initiative, through visits, reunions, telephone calls and letters, in keeping the friendships alive.

Friendship provides support and sustenance but it needs care, continuity and trust in order to survive. It also needs *celebration*. Friends should think up little rewards to celebrate that continuing concern which lies at the heart of friendship. The art of making friends is a talent but it's one that can be acquired. The main thing is to be yourself, let others see you as

90

you are and *not* put on an act. To act the part of somebody you're not takes time and energy and the act very rarely succeeds: people know when we're being real and being phoney, so why bother to pretend that you're something you're not?

In my view women are better at the art of friendship than men. Women are more able to make themselves vulnerable, to discuss intimate areas of their lives and to develop that closeness and empathy which is so essential to friendship. Women are the primary caregivers of infancy, perhaps this gives them the awareness of mutual survival, of interdependency, which is often lacking in men. Men are often, even in friendship, competitive: hence the locker-room camaraderie, the 'mates' of the football or cricket teams to whom a man talks about sport, sex and food. Intimate relations, and feelings, are rarely discussed. Emotions are taboo. Men, slowly, are learning to talk about their feelings, what is going on inside them. Women often find men puzzling; a woman says, 'Let's talk.' (There is so much, the whole of life, to discuss.) A man asks, 'What about?' A man and a woman may sleep in the same bed but that doesn't necessarily mean that they are friends, not if trust, closeness, intimacy are the *sine qua non* of real friendship.

In her book *Intimate Strangers* (Fontana Original) Lillian B. Rubin discusses the relationships between men and women and shows how, for a man, intimacy can be frightening and threatening, recalling his early relationship with his mother from which, because he is male, he has had to separate himself. For the woman, who has not had to experience this loss of emotional closeness, the man's fear of intimacy can be puzzling and confusing and can lead her to feelings of personal rejection and loneliness. Even when she is in bed with her man she may feel that she is not close to him. They are together and yet strangers to each other.

Women, I'm sure, would like to know men better. Men *do* have feelings, but they have been taught not to show them. They have been taught to strive, achieve, *win*. It is the winning, or the need to, that's so destructive. Nobody needs to win in a caring relationship. That relationship is a trade-off, a fair swap, a sharing. There's no winning or losing in caring and sharing. Men fear failure. They need desperately to be No. 1. Men want to have, rather than be. They don't realize that it's OK — it's normal — to fail. None of us is perfect. The success isn't in winning. The success is in being.

91

One of my friends, a woman, has been writing a novel for the past ten years. She gives me one of her looks when I ask her, 'How's the work of art?' She tells me, '*I'm* the work of art.' She is too: kind, warm, generous, humorous. How many men would make such a remark?

Sir Roland Penrose, artist and friend of Picasso, wrote a book called *The Road is Wider than Long*. Its title gives us a clue as to what life is about. It isn't merely about achievement, about winning; it's about enjoying the view and discussing the journey as we go along. What does it matter if you're worth more, financially, than me if you have missed out on the wonder and magic of life? What is the point of being rich and 'successful' if, in the process, you lose your own soul?

A famous psychiatrist asked one of his patients, 'Where is the real you?' The patient was a high-powered executive with a well-known international company. He paused before he answered. 'The real me disappeared some years back,' he said, 'and I haven't seen him since.' The snag about obsessively climbing the ladder of success is that it's very lonely at the top of a ladder. Men may have to put up a front, don a mask, armour themselves to cope with the tough and competitive world in which we live. My advice to men is, when you are with women, let the mask slip. Women understand about vulnerability. They'd rather have that than a false, brash, over-confidence which is the death of intimacy.

Is it possible for men to be friends with women, to have rewarding, platonic relationships with members of the opposite sex? I'd say it was providing that men:

1 *Stop thinking they have no problems and that there's nothing wrong with them.* Many men have this view, which is awful, especially if you happen to be the one who lives with a perfect idiot.

2 *Talk about themselves.* Women appreciate sensitivity and vulnerability. Men are allowed to cry; they don't have to be brave and strong all the time. It can get very boring when men *never* talk about their feelings.

3 *Relax.* Most people lead lives of quiet desperation so that there's no need to pretend that you're happy all the time, successful all the time. Men should stop trying to cover up their real selves and try to be more honest and open about what they think and feel. This, at least, gives women a chance to get to know them.

4 *Take off their emotional armour.* Controlling and manipulating other people is a substitute for caring; it's based on fear, rather than concern. Men should learn that it's OK to feel sad/joyful/miserable/happy/angry/resentful/ecstatic. Most men have an emotional repertoire running from A to B. What women want is the whole person, vulnerability and all. They don't want to have to relate to a cold, unemotional being called — for want of a better name — a man.

Whether it's a man and a man, a woman and a woman, a woman and a man, friendship is absolutely vital to human beings. All of us go through periods of loneliness and there are times when we need to be by ourselves, to lick our wounds, get ourselves together, accept our depression. These are the dark days we all experience. The time for reaching out to the light will come though and it is then that we must show the courage and the real determination that is the prerequisite of forming friendship.

Human beings are dependent on others, even if it's only the milkman. We need others to affirm our reality, to show us respect and affection, to encourage us. To live life without a friend is to dance to the music of life without a partner: you can still enjoy the music but it's so much more enjoyable; so much more fun, when it's shared. The group, not the individual, is the basic unit of human life. Co-operation is more beneficial to our mental well-being than competition.

With friendship we must forget about perfection. If you were perfect, what would you have to talk about? A friend of mine was telling me about this man she'd met who was short, bald and pot-bellied. 'He's far from perfect,' she added, somewhat tautologically. 'Do you want him?' I asked her. 'Madly,' she said. 'I want him as a friend with definite prospects of promotion to lover.' I thought about it.

'Are you willing to put yourself out to get to know this man?' I asked her. 'Out of the window, if necessary,' she said. 'You're not perfect yourself?' I asked. She admitted she wasn't: a very good start. We then planned how she was to invite him to play *Scruples* at her flat. That done, we got down to inventing a board game of our own in which, on square 100, my friend married her man. The first square is marked: 'Say hello.' Everything has to start somewhere.

93

There is nothing complicated about friendship. (It isn't like love, which can be *very* complicated.) The vital points to bear in mind about making — and keeping — friends are:

- *Take the initiative.* Friendships don't just happen. Invite people to coffee, to dinner, to go to the cinema with you. Every week give or accept an invitation, write a letter or telephone somebody just to say hello. Don't, like a child, expect love and attention if you're not willing to give it.
- *Join something.* Do something with others and become involved in other people's lives. This saves you from self-pity and from thinking that you're the only person in the world with problems.
- *If you're really lonely and depressed, go along to see your GP.* Seek help. There is help available in the community and that help may be the first step towards a better life and lasting friendships.
- *Friendship is an essential emotional outlet.* 'The most holy bond of society is friendship,' wrote the feminist writer Mary Wollstonecraft, in the eighteenth century. Sexual love can be marvellous but transitory. The more constant rewards of affection and sympathy between friends are just as important to human beings as the vagaries of passion and love.
- *Don't fear failure in friendship.* Be honest, and be you. Say no if you want, or need, to. Never try to be something you're not. That's unfair on others and on you.
- *Vary your friends.* Don't put all your emotional eggs in one basket. Each friend reflects a different facet of you. Don't expect your friends to be the same: that would mean that you were a one-dimensional person, which you are not.
- *Adopt a more courageous, outgoing and optimistic approach to life.* The prizes go to those who have the courage to take that first step.
- *Start today.* The time to start exercising some control over your own life is today. If you lack encouragement, and that mutual network of support, go out today to the reference library and find out what is going on. Join up, sign on: it's the first step towards making new and rewarding friends.
- *No excuses.* Other people are friendly, if you give them a chance. The loneliness many of us suffer is often self-inflicted. It's up to each and every one of us to break that pattern of loneliness by reaching out to others.

94

● *Never try to be perfect*. Who needs *that*? Be bold, have
courage. The first step is the worst.

Years ago, I met a woman at a bus stop. 'Hello,' I said. We
started chatting, about this and that. I told her I was very short-
sighted. On subsequent meetings I used to greet her by saying,
'Hello, beautiful, can you tell me the way to the optician's?' I've
known her now for some twelve years and we are still very good,
close friends. We talk to each other about the bad times and the
good times. We hide nothing from each other. There's no sex in
the relationship; I think that would have altered the whole thing.
Friendship is — to me — a holy bond and it has provided in my
own life rich and rewarding experiences which I value as much
as my passionate loves.

Lovers may come and go. Friends, if we work at the
relationship and water the beautiful flower of friendship, stay
forever.

Chapter 8
Sex and love

With sex, a great deal depends on individual preference, place, time and mood. What turns you on may well repel me; what you find disgusting I may find exciting (and vice versa). The main thing is to realize that, with sex, there's no accounting for taste. I once met a man who became sexually aroused whenever he saw a safety pin open. His sexual turn-on was strange, but inexpensive. I met a man once who told me, 'My wife likes sex.' He said it with disgust and horror. I was so shocked that I bought him a drink as he sat down and told me the details. My own view is that sex is different things to different people. It can be a source of great happiness – or distress.

In theory, we have moved on from Victorian times when sex was a taboo subject. No respectable woman in those days had affairs, no unmarried woman was expected to be anything else but chaste and pure. Now, in theory, women can have sexual freedom: the pill has released them from fear of pregnancy, they can do the choosing, if they wish, as far as sexual partners are concerned; it is generally accepted that women have sexual feelings; many women, with men, insist upon a recognition of themselves as sexual beings.

This should all be for the best. Sex is now spoken of, discussed, accepted as an important element in personal happiness. This should be a good time for men and women. They should be happier, more contented, with their sex lives. Sex is no longer taboo. With a greater social tolerance of the sexual needs of both men and women there should now be a prevailing sense that women and men are on the way to mutual understanding, respect and well-being.

Judging by the letters I receive at *Cosmopolitan* (which are mostly about sex or love) and looking at the lives of friends and acquaintances, this clearly is not the case. Many people don't enjoy their sex lives; many women find it difficult to cope with

96

the roles foisted on them by men (sex goddess, housewife, maid, madonna, temptress, good mother – sometimes all at the same time). Women have a feeling that they are being sold short by the present emphasis on health and sex. There is plenty of discussion about G spots, multiple orgasms, the techniques of sex, but what about *feelings, emotional involvement, intimacy*?

Have women really gained sexual freedom? Let's consider one or two aspects of the situation that suggest that the pressures on women are different from Victorian times, but that they are there, nevertheless. When William Blake visited his garden of love he didn't find a place to fulfil his joys and desires: what he found was a sign saying *Thou shalt not*. It's rather like that, nowadays, for women. Let me give a few examples.

1 *Thou shalt not be TOO sexy*. Victorian men divided women into respectable ladies and harlots. Modern men don't do that. Or do they? If a married man these days has an affair then – providing he's discreet – he can get away with it. If a married woman has an affair, her husband may get very angry indeed. What's sauce for the goose isn't sauce for the gander. If a man flirts with other women he's 'a bit of a lad'. If a woman with a partner shows interest in other men she risks being branded as 'wild', or 'a slut', or even 'a prostitute'. Often, the man who flirts is the first one to take umbrage when his partner does the same thing.

2 *Thou shalt not talk about feelings to men*. All men have mothers. In order to become men, males have to break away from their mothers, establish their own space, throw away childish – and motherly – things. For many grown men this means that when they are with *any* woman, they feel afraid: that they will be eaten by the woman, swamped by her emotions; drawn back to a state of dependency and helplessness. It's not true that men don't have feelings. They are simply frightened to express them. They are afraid that they will betray their dependency, vulnerability, inadequacy. The truth is that most women understand these feelings of vulnerability: for a woman, intimacy, togetherness, closeness are an important part of sex and love. Solution? Every time a woman meets a man she fancies, she should wear a T-shirt on which is printed the message: I AM NOT YOUR MOTHER. Men have a deep fear of being psychologically eaten alive by women. So much for the

vaunted equality of the sexes in the last decade of the twentieth century.

3 *Thou shalt not be cherished*. Men are keen on sex, but not so keen on love; women are keen on sex within the context of love. 'Making love' means little shows of affection: looking, touching, stroking, tender words of endearment, cuddling, gentle biting, stroking the hair and other parts of the body. It means taking your time and enjoying all the stops along the way. Sex can be two minutes of squelchy noises or an ecstatic experience. The statistics concerning 'making love' show that 44 per cent of couples spend 'up to half an hour' enjoying love. Some 3 per cent of the population (lucky blighters!) claim to prolong the act of love for hours on end. For the majority, however, 'making love' can last any time from 3 *seconds* (my italics – this is worthy of the Keystone Cops), 3 minutes to 30 minutes. So much for sex in practice. No wonder one woman told me that she would rather have a ham sandwich! If music be the food of love what many women experience is a tin whistle.

4 *Thou shalt not do it your way*. Looking at the media (popular newspapers, magazines and *some* series on TV), you would gather that people are indulging in sex every minute of the day. The average man and woman in this country (you are told) has sex every 3·8 days. If you are between the ages of 16 and 24 you will have sex every 2·5 days. These figures are likely to strike despondency and a feeling of failure in your heart, especially if you read those papers and magazines in which people seem to have sex, or at least be thinking of sex, all the time. This, plus the myriad sex manuals now freely available, leads many women (and a few men) to ask in bed not 'Do you love me?', but 'How do I rate?' This is the age of the Sexual Olympics, sex as a competition, which leaves you and I feeling we're Third Division stuff compared with all those people who do it 3·8 times per week, and probably swing from chandeliers at the same time. The truth? Do what *you* enjoy and do it when *you* want to. Comparisons are odious. The average man (and woman) is a myth. There are only individuals, then couples. What they do together is their own business. There are many couples who have sex less than once a month (and some who don't have sex at all) *and are still happy*. Sex isn't compulsory. Nor is it a test of stamina. You're supposed to enjoy it, not feel pressure upon you to keep up with the ratings.

5 *Though shalt not relax*. It is interesting that, now the AIDS threat has altered most people's attitude towards casual sex, one night stands and passing affairs, *some* women feel a sense of relief. 'Thank goodness casual sex is out,' a woman told me recently, 'For me, sex doesn't work without love and now you just have to know a person very well before you sleep with him, don't you? There's no question of sleeping around. I'm glad, you know. I've tried that and I never got anything out of it. Thank heavens we can all relax and take things a bit more slowly. That suits me fine. I'm for love. I dislike condoms and that cold mechanical attitude towards sex. I'll just have to be chaste until Mr Right comes along and I don't mind at all.' Now, for men and women it's all right to say no. For some people that takes off the pressure of keeping up with the sex-obsessed Joneses.

There is no evidence to suggest that woman are less interested in sex than men. Nor is there any evidence to suggest that women are more emotional, unpredictable and suggestible than men. Women, like men, can be aggressive, rational, dominant, intelligent and sexy. Freud asked a colleague, Marie Bonaparte, 'What do women want?' MB didn't answer: she knew Freud's views on women (he thought they were ' a great mystery'). What women want, like men, is fulfilling experiences. They want the best of everything − a good life, a sense of achievement, good experiences. There's no mystery about women, except in the hearts of men who are prejudiced against them.

There are differences, though, in the way in which men approach sex and love. Love = sex plus friendship and love within a relationship are very important to women. For many men there *is* a competitive aspect to sex. They like to be 'good at it', they are interested in quantity, not quality, they can be very possessive with their partners and feel that if a woman is attracted to somebody else it is a reflection on their sexual virility. (It may well be a symptom of something quite different, including the partner's personality or attitude to life, or ability to be close and intimate, all of which are important to women.)

Consider the following letter sent to me at 'On The Couch'. It illustrates, I think, some of the different attitudes that men and women have about sex:

I don't feel like making love very often. To me, a couple of times a month, spontaneously, with lots of foreplay, is great

— a treat to be savoured. Kisses and cuddles and doing things together is enough for me to know how much I love him. He is sweet, kind, attractive, in fact all the things I want from a partner and we have lived together through thick and thin for the last three years.

My boyfriend is, at present, insanely jealous because he thinks — as I don't make love to him all the time — that I must be having an affair with somebody else. Why can't I make him understand that I only want him?

It's simply that I don't regard sex as being as important as the rest of the human race seem to think it is. Please, tell me if there is anything I can do to want to make love more often before I go through any more cross-questioning about who-I-have-been-having-an-affair-with-this-week.

Poor guy, he really thinks that I no longer find him attractive and that just isn't true.

Here is my reply. I've included it in full because it leads us on to sex-and-love-as-one, which I think is the answer to so much misery:

Dear J. The best way to think of women's sexuality is to think of the moon: it waxes and wanes, ebbs and flows; it's cyclical and part and parcel of life, and love. A man's sexuality is more immediate; like the sun it doesn't change, it burns and glows and is always there, rising and setting each day. For a woman, sex is an aspect of love; for a man, love is an aspect, sometimes a very baffling one, of sex.

Women, baptized in the waters of love, know the sea won't run dry. The ocean of love is very deep and many quite beautiful fish swim in its waters. This is why, for a woman, touching, looking, stroking, whispering, cuddling are all part of that magic sea. This is why women say, 'Just hold me.' There are many, many times when they want *love* — not sex.

For a man the prevailing philosophy is *use it or lose it*. Many men see cuddling, hugging and touching not as — with the right person — lovely things to do in their own right, but as a means to an end. The end, of course, is to get into bed. There, the man can prove yet again, to himself, that he is a man. This is the pathetic 'phallusy' and an extremely sad one. There are many rooms in the mansion of love; most men spend their time in the basement.

100

Once men are into phallic power (and possession) they brutalize what love is all about. It is about magic and sharing: not bossiness, laying down the law or wanting to own someone. 'I had him/her' is a horrible phrase. 'We made love to each other' is so much better. You can make love to someone with your eyes, your voice, by holding hands. You don't have to be in bed; you can make love by saying something encouraging to a woman when she's not looking her best, has her hair in curlers or is washing the dishes. It's all part of the magic of love.

Take possession – that's not love at all – nor is jealousy. I get a lot of letters about jealousy and all I can say is that it's a very destructive emotion indeed. Your boyfriend is playing a very dangerous game by wanting to own you, check your movements. You cannot imprison love. No box is large enough to contain the ocean.

I suggest you buy some sand from a builders' merchant. Take a handful of the sand and show your man that when you grasp it tight, squeeze it, try to imprison it in your grasp, it merely runs away. Keep your hand open, hold it very gently, let it be and the sand will stay in your palm. It's the same with love. Love is caring, not possession.

Since jealousy is a very dangerous emotion, I suggest that you point out to your man that he risks losing the love you feel for him if he persists in projecting his own insecurities and fears on to you. He must learn to gain his identity and confidence in ways other than being your sexual landlord.

Let's get back to your libido. If having sex a couple of times a month is enough for you, it is. It doesn't mean that you're a sexual dyslexic, that you need pills or potions or hormone tablets or high doses of vitamin E. It doesn't mean that you should have your smell checked out in case you're not sniffing the pheromones. It just means you're you: with your own wants and needs.

Whilst you want to swim in the ocean of love your man wants to constantly dive into the shallow waters of sex. You are going to have to do something about it. Perhaps you might join the Love Maniacs Club which I'm thinking of starting (Sex Maniacs down the hall) which will spend long evenings just drinking wine and talking about love.

Your man should change his tactics completely, and whisk you away to the Cotswolds (or Brighton) – I always think that hotel bedrooms are potent aphrodisiacs — then subject you to foreplay of the greatest finesse. When you are absolutely mad for sex, he should then say, 'Let's go for a walk/cold shower.' It could be his insistence on sex that's putting you off.

The best aphrodisiacs are always psychological. Go to your favourite places, walk in the rain/through woods together, go window shopping. Laugh together, talk together, make love (ie, whisper and cuddle together) as much as you can. Forget sex for two minutes. Then, that feeling of wanting to give yourself, be very, very close will spring out of what you are, what you mean to each other. That's real sex. That's when sex and love blend into one. Once you get that the chances are you'll want more of it.

For you, don't say, 'Sex is over here, love is over there.' Sex is — or should be — a beautiful part of love. For him, don't let him think that, when you have sex, it's like a a bi-monthly reward for being abstemious. You shouldn't be lying there, thinking of England, faking orgasms or anything else. You should both be relaxing and enjoying each other's company in all sorts of ways. When you've learned to do that the sex will look after itself.

More nonsense is written about sex than anything else. When Kinsey announced that couples had sex 2·4 times per week the whole Western world was full of exhausted couples trying to keep a respectable place on the Richter Scale. (Whilst I was steadily working at the ·4.) This figure is an average: it presumably includes couples who have sex twice a year. There are no norms as to how often you should have sex: thank God, sex isn't — like taxes — compulsory; sex was, and is, meant to be shared and enjoyed as part of love.

You are, therefore, J., quite normal. Please tell your man I said so. Tell him, too, that your weekly fantasy lovers exist only in his head because he can't understand why you aren't like him. Tell him about the moon, the ocean, love. Don't be indignant with him; just tell him, quietly, who you are, what you value most.

He, if he loves you, will respect your needs and cease reciting the alphabet of love as though it ran from A to F. Tell him to save energy and make love slowly.

When two people come together in love there is care and compassion and generosity; there is laughter and seriousness,

102

commitment and freedom. There is no faking, or possession or making demands. What we give, we give freely. There is no jealousy or possession. Tell him I told you.

Every woman has a bottom drawer of the things she wants. With J., she has to tell her man what her needs are. If they need help in discussing their problems they can go to Marriage Guidance or go to their GP and ask to be referred to a sex counsellor. Often, though, the misunderstandings between men and women can be solved by real caring and sharing *on both sides*. It takes two to tango and it takes two people who really care about each other to get sexual — and other problems — into perspective. The main thing is to *say something* (or to get professional help, if needed), hold the problem up to the light where both can see it, name it and do something about it.

I'm not underestimating the problems that arise when a man and a woman fall in love. With friendship we can be open and honest, be ourselves (that's what friendship is about). With love each of the two people in love seems to bring a host of fantasies/wish-fulfilments/past defeats with him or her. Each partner carries a large bag of expectations which he wants the Loved One to fulfil. Some of the fantasies can be very strange indeed; some of the expectations can be quite unrealistic.

To understand love you have to know something about the unconscious mind, about dreams and daydreams, memory and desire. You have to know that the unconscious mind is selfish. It obeys no rules, transcends time and space, rolls towards the shore of the conscious psyche with the incessant murmur: *gimmee, gimmee, gimmee*. The motto of the UCS (the Unconscious) is: I WANT IT NOW.

It is not only the unconscious mind that causes mischief when two people fall in love. Take imprinting. There was a Tom and Jerry cartoon in which a chicken follows Tom around and says to him, 'You're my mummy.' There were also Konrad Lorenz's goslings who followed *him* around (the famous ethologist had become mummy to them simply because he was the first moving object they saw after hatching). Do human beings imprint? Does some special characteristic of a person make somebody else fall in love with that person? Does this help to explain why some people attach themselves to the most unsuitable partners? Does it help to explain why some men, despite rational evidence to the contrary, insist on seeing their partners as their mummies?

103

Sailing on the ocean of love, around the Isle of U in the unconscious mind, are all the people we've ever met and loved. They are dressed as brigands, demons, the good father, the good mother, princes and princesses. When you fall in love with somebody you project these images on to that person. The past comes along to interfere with the present.

She falls in love with him because he reminds her of her father; he falls in love with her because she reminds him of his mother. When people fall in love — and something goes wrong, it doesn't work out — the pain is indescribable. It feels like a child feels who is abandoned. Love is very important to human beings. When you love you invest the Loved One with the love of the present and the loves of the past. That's an enormous investment, a powerful wish fulfilment, and it feels absolutely unbearable when those dreams and wish fulfilments turn to ashes.

Love needn't always be sexual, but there's always an 'M' factor (Magic, Magnetism, Mystery; does she love him because he has a moustache like her father? Does he love her because she's plump and homely like his mother?). The unconscious mind isn't interested in reason, only in images. Given a suitable image — a suitable trigger — all your love goes, whoosh, on to one person. You hang the multi-coloured coat of your dreams on to one peg and away you go on your voyage of love. Love makes you vulnerable (with all those dreams at stake) and many people can and do get hurt, terribly. Consider the following two cases:

Case 1. Jane falls in love with Barry. It is the real thing. The symptoms, from which both suffer, are a minor nervous breakdown, shaky hands, loss of appetite, an ache in the solar plexus and a delusion that the sun is shining even when it's raining. Jane is beautiful (everybody says so). Barry is fat, bald and with a homely face (to say the least). That doesn't seem to make much difference to Jane. Love isn't so much blind as short-sighted. Cupid, that endomorphic trouble maker, doesn't care where he fires his arrows. To Jane, Barry is her prince. She loves him.

The two have four months of bliss together, then things start to go wrong. Jane starts to impose conditions on Barry: she will love him more *if* he talks to her more, shows more affection to her, cleans the bath after using it, wears his grey leather jacket more, cuddles her more, holds her more. What Jane wants — although she doesn't know it — is to be treated like a little girl might be treated by her father: to be protected, loved, adored (that's fine). She also wants *all* her fantasies fulfilled (that isn't; that's unreasonable but who said that the unconscious mind was reasonable?).

They start to quarrel. They kiss and make up. She begins to behave badly: to demand more of his time, his life, his love. She became possessive about him, didn't like him looking at attractive women on TV and commenting that they looked pretty. She wanted him all to herself.

Nobody can live like that. People need space, need to breathe. The UCS doesn't. What it wants, it wants now. What he wanted was *safety*. He didn't see, stealing ashore, the whore, the milkmaid, the pirates. The relationship had become a mess. He couldn't cope with her wants; she couldn't give him what he needed. The ship of love had been boarded by figures from the past, all of them shouting I WANT.

When two people make love there are four people present: there's the her in him and the him in her. That's fine. It's when there are six (or sixty-six) in the same bed that the trouble starts — all those shadowy figures, making trouble, just when you think you've made it, just the two of you, together.

Is there no way out of this identity confusion? For Jane and Barry there wasn't. Neither of them were playing safe, but neither of them were sure who had landed on the shore. Not being certain, having no clear idea of what they *most* wanted from each other, their love was destined to fail. Whose fault was it?

Case 2. He married a mummy figure, Mother Courage. She married the Little Boy Lost. It worked very well until the first child came along and he found that he wasn't the sole recipient of her attention and love. He started to act petulantly. She started to say things to him like, 'Why don't you grow up?' Nasty question. He'd married her in order to avoid that very requirement.

What she had originally wanted was not what she wanted now. They had never argued when they first married (little boys don't argue with mummy), but now they argued all the time. He hadn't changed, but she *had*. She wanted, when she first met him, a little boy: somebody to look after. She got just that.

Now, a mother, she wanted a man (or, unconsciously, a prince). He didn't fulfil that specification. She wanted somebody she could talk to, have adventures with, rely on, look up to, respect. 'Why aren't you more of a man?' she asked him. He was a man but the wrong sort of man for her: she'd changed.

When her son was 5 years old, and at school, she found a part-time job and met a man in the office she could talk to. Whoosh. She fell in love with him (right specification; more suitable trigger) and that was the end of the marriage. Whose fault was it? It may be a mistake to marry a 'safe' partner. Who says that the partner's going to stay that way (or that what you want now is what you'll want in five/ten years time?) All the time, in the unconscious mind, the waves lap on the shore and the cry is heard: *Gimmee, gimmee, I want it now.*

For the man, it was tragic. For him, it was like being abandoned by his mother. He'd been through bliss, image making, a comfortable love (safe in each other's fantasies) and now there was a failure of the dream and the end of love. He was what he was. Is love always so dangerous and painful? Does it always have to end in pain?

I don't believe so. Your unconscious mind *may* see your partner as a prince/princess/mother/father/skivvy/demon. The conscious mind, however, is powerful too. It is in touch with reality and can constantly test out reality and keep a lookout for the tricks of the unconscious. *The conscious mind is capable of seeing the Loved One as a real person.* This is the key to a more successful, more enjoyable, painless love.

It doesn't mean that you can't share fantasies together, but those fantasies have to be agreed, discussed, mutual. They're not projections of one partner's needs, wishes (or fears) on the other. They add to, rather than diminish, the mutual affection and regard for each other.

Love is part of the beauty of the world. Love is life. Human beings need to love and be loved. You can love Jesus (for believers, this is a safe love, with a promise of forgiveness) or love children/animals/the countryside/your car. Whatever you love, love is vital to you. How do you tune in to the music of love and make it to safety, joy and ecstasy with another human being? It's what most of us want, so how do you and I achieve it? The vital things to remember about love are:

● *It exists.* Love is the Beatles, your favourite tune, walking

106

with someone who is very special, holding hands. Even though it seems as though the world's falling apart, it's still love that makes the world go round. Life is flat and dreary without love.

- *You can fall in love any time, any place, any age.* Your heart can go whoosh at a bus-stop, in a lift or at Heathrow, when you're flying to Spain and he (that 'certain someone') is, curses, in the queue for Paris.

- *Love is a trade-off.* As in any trade-off, you can cheat or be honest. I think you should *never* tell lies, make false promises, fail to know just what you mean to each other, what the agreement is. You don't need it in writing. You do need to feel you're not being used, manipulated. Honesty is a vital part of trading your heart.

- *Love is equality.* The prince and princess reign, as equals, in the kingdom of love. They have choice over who to let into their kingdom. Pirates will enter the kingdom only if you allow them. The ship they sail on is called POWER. Power is nothing to do with love.

- *A person you love shares your dreams.* Love doesn't mean no fantasies. Love is best when fantasies match, coincide: not when they're absent. Talk about your dreams, your fantasies.

- *We have to be aware of the irrational, destructive elements in love.* They are nothing to do with that person you're opposite now, and love. Seize the happiness of the present: this is the best antidote for the pain of the past. Don't use your love to re-work, sort out, the past, that would be unfair. The person you love is real, so treat him/her with respect and courtesy, not as your analyst/father/mother.

- *Love takes courage.* When I'm old I'll still have the courage to believe in love. I'm not particularly brave: I just want something good to remember when my last day comes. To prepare myself for old age (and my pink beret phase) I intend to get as much practice as I can, now, in being courageous. You'd need something heavy to stop me believing in love.

- *Love is life.* You may not have love, you may have lost your love and been terribly hurt but when you stop believing in love something in you dies. It's not going to die in me.

- *Love is risk.* The pleasure and the pain await us and nobody can say which we'll get and in what amounts. I'm willing to take that risk, come what may. Love is a great adventure.

- *Love is percentages*. In love, you may have it all. If you
  don't, why not settle for 70 per cent, which seems a
  reasonable percentage to me. If you have the warmth, the
  contact comfort, the friendship (and the lust) but he/she
  isn't *exactly* what you want, settle for the percentage that's
  important to you and, through open and honest
  negotiation, work on the rest. Love has to be worked at. It
  comes out of the blue, but it has to be nurtured when your
  feet eventually touch the ground.

I once met a woman who told me that she had never, in 25
years of marriage, had a quarrel with her husband. 'We're still
like a couple of kids,' she said, 'still romantic.' Whatever image
each had of the other, it worked. I met a couple, too, who still
love each other after 30 years. 'We don't have sex,' they told me.
'We're past it, but we have lots of cuddles and that's enough for
us.' She was 50; he was 55.

With love (and sex) there's no accounting for taste. What you
have to stop believing is that other people do it better (or
more) than you. They do it how (and when) they want to do it
and so must you. You must love – and have sex – in your own
style.

A central concept in this area of life is *respect*. If you respect
someone you treat them as a real person, an equal, a person who
wants the good things in life: fulfilment and pleasure, not
indignity, callous manipulation and pain.

If you are a man, you shouldn't imagine that women are
masochistic and enjoy pain. They do not. *Some* men enjoy
inflicting pain and some women, as a result of a violent
childhood, lack of love, discouragement and abandonment, the
loss of self-esteem, are masochistic, but this is a tiny minority.
Most women don't want to find themselves in a mad dance of
pain with a man.

If you are a woman and find that your man is hurting you,
realize that this is not right and look hard at the alternatives. If
you choose to stay with that man, understand why. Likewise, if
you choose to go, understand why. Women do have a choice. A
woman does not have to stay with a man who continually robs
her of her self-esteem.

Women, with love and sex, should:

- *Have a 'me' time*. You may enjoy making other people
  happy, including men. That's fine but don't forget about

time out for you, for your needs, your goals. Don't become dependent upon a man for your self-esteem, because that is dangerous. Live your life in the round.

- *Be more self-assertive.* You don't have to express yourself entirely through, or with the permission of, a man. If you have a family, use it as a safe base from which to lead your life, but remember that the family is not your whole life; you have a duty towards other women, and the world outside.

- *Refuse to take all the blame.* If it rains on the picnic, don't take the blame and don't suppose it rained because women were born to suffer. You do have some choice. Your way out of the mess is to find people who understand the hell you are in and will support you and encourage you on that step-by-step journey back to self-esteem.

- *Be sensible.* If there is something wrong with your sex life that is spoiling your relationship with your man, seek help. Go to marriage guidance, go along and see your GP, ask for an appointment with a sex counsellor.

- *Respect themselves.* Single women who indulge in casual sex should carry condoms. Only a fool these days would indulge in casual sex without adequate protection against sexually transmitted diseases, including AIDS. Only a fool or somebody who didn't respect herself.

Violence, hate and harmful attitudes generally towards sex can only be cured by an insistence on the part of us all that we respect each other more. Women are not more caring, gentler, more nurturing, more loving than men. Men can learn to be like that, men can learn to be more loving, but that means that women will have to go out in to society, where men are, and preach a more humane message about human relationships. Men must learn to contribute more to the home: to child rearing, to the family, to being caring and sharing parents.

When large numbers of women are in parliament, when there are large numbers of female judges, architects, trade union leaders, captains of industry, heads of schools, doctors and dentists (and all those other professions at present dominated by men), then the love and sex lives of men and women *will* change. When men really do something about that vital question in any family – who minds the children? – and learn to express the more vulnerable and tender side of themselves, that will be a marvellous time for men and women.

109

As men and women do become more equal in society, so the quality of all our lives will change. Love, then, between a man and a woman will be marvellous, as will sex. For both work best in a context of real friendship, of true equality, real concern for each other and sharing the good and the bad. I look forward to that time. I believe in love. I believe that men *and* women need love but love − true love − is only possible where there is equality and respect between a man and a woman.

Chapter 9
Marriage

I adore weddings. Whether it is to be held in a church or a registry office, I never turn down an invitation to see two people promise, from henceforth, to re-write the script of their lives and live together as one. The words of the church service are quite beautiful: 'to have and to hold from this day forward, for better for worse, for richer for poorer, in sickness and in health, to love and to cherish, till death us do part'.

Ritual and ceremony are very important, very comforting, to human beings. In a society starved of both, a wedding is a big occasion, a dramatic act, a rite of passage in which two individuals vow to construe their lives as a couple, to change from the I to the We. Will though love, honour and serve your partner, sick or well, forsaking all others, keep thee only to that partner? It's quite a promise to make. Most people make it. Marriage is still very popular. About 95 per cent of women and 90 per cent of men marry before the age of 40. It's *staying* married that seems to be becoming more and more difficult.

What are the facts on marriage? There has been a decrease in teenage marriages, and in marriages of younger women (20–24 year olds). By and large, people are marrying later. There has been an increase in cohabitation – couples living together without benefit of marriage; there has been, since the 1970s, a quite remarkable increase in divorce. Since the Divorce Reform Act of 1971, the divorce rate in this country has doubled; Britain, together with Denmark, has the highest divorce rate in Europe. It is estimated that one in three of marriages are heading for dissolution. Why should this be?

I think it is to do with the changing nature of marriage, with the higher expectations of women and with misunderstandings between men and woman as to what marriage is and what it should provide. Marriage is a tough business but, it should be remembered, two-thirds of marriages last. What is it that keeps

111

a couple together and what is it that makes them decide to part? This is something that deserves careful thought, if only to mitigate the misery of the 160,000 children involved in divorce proceedings in England and Wales each year.

Let's look at the nature of marriage. There was no mystery about the marriage of my own father and mother. Each had a very specific role. My father went to work every morning about 6.30 am, and returned each evening about 6 pm. For six days a week, he went off to work on the land as a labourer. It was a great luxury for him when, later on, he only had to work for half a day on Saturday. As with God, Sunday was his day of rest (even then he worked in the garden). He started work at the age of 12, retired aged 65. He died the same year, having worked all his life. That is what men did.

My mother stayed at home, looking after the children. She changed nappies, took the babies out (my father never pushed a pram in his life − men didn't). She did the washing, cooked, cleaned the house. It was a far from idyllic scenario. My mother, I realize with hindsight, was often depressed. Her role was the one of home-maker: it was often a lonely, hard and thankless task. She was the mother, housewife and source of affection in the family. She was the child-minder, the carer.

This *instrumental* model of marriage in which each partner has a very clear job demarcation was the norm in my boyhood (and had been the norm for many years before that). It was the one I was brought up on, experienced, knew. My parents saw little of each other; my father was very close to his brothers, my mother to her sisters. My parents spent very little time in each other's company and my own theory is that I − and my brothers and sisters − were all conceived on a Sunday afternoon when the older siblings were at Sunday school. It was a kind of marriage: my father was the boss, the provider; my mother looked after him and his children.

Compare modern marriage. I'm a long-married man myself. I learned − the hard way − that what is needed in marriage is adaptability and flexibility. The central question in marriage is: does it work? If that way of behaving, those attitudes, those rigid roles don't bring sufficient rewards to both partners, they must be modified or scrapped. This is easy enough to say, but the divorce figures testify that it is not so easy to do.

These days, every woman I know wants the same from marriage: (a) an equal partnership in which there is no boss; (b) equality in status, decision-making, discussion, communication, power; (c) a relationship based on sharing rather than 'hand-outs'; (d) a relationship in which the woman is treated with respect, as a human being and an equal, rather than as a sex object.

However, women want more than this. They also look to their partners for *intimacy* (ie, a feeling of being close, loving, caring, as one; *friendship* (a feeling of being able to talk to someone, trust them, have fun with them, share intimacies, support them, be supported by them); *love* (which isn't just two minutes − or even half an hour − of sex but which includes self-revelation, affection, vilnerability, touching, emotional support, tenderness). A woman wants to feel emotionally close to her spouse, and for him to be not a boss, or a sole provider, but a true friend. This *companionship* model of marriage makes many more demands than does the instrumental. Many men, in particular, find it difficult to cope with. Why?

There are five main reasons:

1   *Change.* Instrumental marriage is easier for men. They may have seen it in their own parents' marriage, with clear, defined roles, people knowing where they stood: the man is the head of the family and the purpose of the family is to raise children (which are primarily the mother's responsibility). Companion-ship marriage involves change (which is not easy for all human beings to cope with). It is a dynamic, growing, emergent partnership between two human beings. There is no set script: the couple write their own script of life, together, as they go along. Men *may* see this as an awesome − and unrewarding − task.

2   *Ghosts from the past.* Each partner may bring to the marriage, and act out in the here and now, emotional conflicts which they have experienced in childhood. If men are very reluctant to talk about themselves, and their feelings, these conflicts may continue to be acted out, like a tape recorder playing the same tape over and over again.

3   *Mistaken identity.* One of the major ghosts from the past is the man's mother. He may treat his wife as his mother rather than as a real person, an equal partner. Growing up for men involves breaking the dependency link with the mother. Not

113

all men achieve this successfully. Some men will simply transfer to their partners these dependency needs; others will fear intimacy, since being too close to one's partner implies being too close to mother or the equivalent of psychological regression (and a resurrection of those feelings of dependency/vulnerability/helplessness generated by closeness). The man is, unconsciously, saying, 'You are my mother. I don't want to be too dependent on you or you will fragment/destroy me.' This isn't rational, but it is a very real fear in some men.

4 *Splitting*. A man, in repressing his identification with his mother, represses the erotic/affectional components of that identification. He will see his mother as an 'ideal' person, rather than a real person. He may go on to divide all women into two kinds: women who are mothers (who are ideal); women who can arouse him erotically (bad women, whores). This is why some men are shocked when their wives behave erotically, are frank about their sexual needs, or make demands sexually. Since women have higher sexual expectations from marriage these days, they may be puzzled that the husband doesn't behave erotically with them and, more, seems to have a positive fear of intimacy. (For a brilliant description of the reasons *why* men fear intimacy read Lillian B. Rubin's *Intimate Strangers*, Fontana, in which she discusses relationships between men and women and men's dependency needs.) For many men, sex is lust, even within a marriage. It is something apart from his – often genuine – love of his wife. For a woman, sex and love go together. For a man, it is hard for sex and love to go together: to put it simply, sex is something 'naughty' and love is painful when it is not idealized because it interferes with his fantasies about his mother, and women in general. Sex is no problem to many men; it is love which causes them confusion.

5 *Verbal facility*. Women, in general, find it easier to talk about themselves than men. Women talk to each other; men *do* things together. A man will often say to another man, 'What do those women find to talk *about*?' The answer is, of course, that the women are talking about life, their feelings, relationships, their children, whatever. With men, the conversation may be limited to sport, food, sex: a proscribed list of subjects (which does not include inner feelings). If women, in a companionship marriage, have higher expectations from their men regarding the sharing of confidences/discussion of feelings/admissions of

114

vulnerability, they may be expecting something from men that they find very difficult. Whether this gap in verbal facility between men and women is innate or the result of social conditioning is unknown. Some men acquire the skills, which suggests men can improve their ability to express their needs and feelings verbally if they practise — and receive encouragement for so doing.

This paints a somewhat depressing scenario, and you may be thinking, by now, that there is not much hope for companionship marriage if such tricky problems have to be overcome. However, the alternative to companionship marriage — the instrumental — seems to me like the alternative to old age. Looking back, I would call my parents' marriage a contract; they hardly knew each other, weren't going anywhere, had few aspirations. Every marriage today has the *chance* of being a real partnership of two people, a relationship which *can* bring fun, true friendship and plenty of emotional rewards.

Marriage can provide you with children, more money (single parents are mostly poorer than the rest of us), and sharing. Hopefully, marriage means there is somebody who remains constant, who always backs you even when others are against you. It can provide affection and regular cuddles (just as important to women as regular sex); sharing the good and the bad; emotional support and the pleasures of companionship.

The sharing and companionship, plus that feeling of empathy and closeness, are vital. Most women who abandon their marriages, don't do so because of sex. 'I couldn't talk to him any more,' they say, or 'I never felt close to him.' It is this loss of *oneness*, of friendship, that destroys many marriages.

It is true that marriage entails a loss of freedom, but then for every single choice in life we make, there is a price. If we choose A and B, we can't have C and D. If we opt for marriage, we do give up our option of acting like a single person, having only ourselves to please, doing what we like, when we like. Marriage, however, needn't be a prison. The couple concerned can allow each other adequate space, they can interact differently at different times and negotiate on important issues. Let's have a look at some of the mistakes and the emotional conflicts within that popular institution called marriage.

In the first five years of marriage couples have to try to adjust to each other, so it is a critical time for them both and, needless to say, there is a high incidence of divorce during this period. This may be due to one partner being over-authoritarian, or clinging to old patterns, or to resentment *vis-à-vis* real, or imagined, lack of freedom. The question of *psychological space* is crucial; being married doesn't mean that each partner has to live in the other's pocket; it doesn't mean that one partner is totally dependent on the other or that the two should live in a stifling, exclusive relationship. In a good marriage there will be his space, her space and shared space. The amount of shared space will vary from time to time within a marriage; it will vary from marriage to marriage to suit the dependency needs of the couple concerned; there should always be some area in which each of the partners can say, 'This is mine.'

The term 'space' doesn't mean that her space is the kitchen and his is the garage; it doesn't mean that she looks after the cooking and the housework, whilst he is concerned with world affairs and worries about China. It means a dynamic interaction in which roles are allocated, dependency needs catered for, needs for freedom and independence are met and the couple decide what sort of relationship the marriage involves. A woman may want more closeness, more shared space (ie, psychological space); a man may yearn to go down to the pub to have a drink with his mates (less shared space). The *negotiation of space* is one of the vital elements within marriage, and one which is very difficult to get right. The Duchess of Windsor said of her husband, the Duke: 'I married him for better or worse, but not for lunch.' Even they, a very close and intimate couple, had some time away from each other, time in which she could chat with her friends, 'do her own thing'. The Duchess of Windsor's boundary maintenance concerned lunch-time, but it isn't always as simple and clear cut as that. Sometimes a partner may feel that she/he has sufficient physical space, but that her/his psychological space is being invaded when she or he is with the partner. Consider the following letter to 'On The Couch':

I've been married five years. I met my husband when I was 19 and fell head over heels in love with him. Deep down I love him intensely but our constant personality clashes make me very depressed. We have a happy 2-year-old daughter and my husband adores her. In fact, he's a caring, loving and involved father.

But he's a perfectionist, while I'm a bumbling, head-in-the-

116

clouds idealist. Lately he's started to comment on my accent, my dress and how I act in public. This hurts me. To me, these things are me, just like the nose on my face.

I sometimes feel the essence of me is being destroyed drop by drop from a niggling, nagging tap. I have phases where I try to change; I try not to interpret every comment as a personal attack but it always slides back into a full-blown confrontation.

By the way, I'm not a stay-at-home mum. I work part-time, am involved in politics, play badminton, etc. I try not to have time for self-pity.

I'd like to do something positive, but what?

Here is my reply:

Dear X. Some time ago, when I used to drive, I gave a lift to a young woman who was hitching. When I'd stopped, she asked, 'Can my friends come too?' Out of the hedge stepped another woman and two unshaven young men. I was grateful she didn't have her mother there too!

In family terms this is known as the *hidden agenda*: what comes up once you've tied the knot, the fantasies we bring with us into the marriage and the games we start to play once we've settled for wedded bliss.

The best book on the subject is *Families and How to Survive Them* by Robin Skynner and John Cleese (Methuen). Skynner, a distinguished family therapist, and John Cleese really do give some marvellous insights into the roles that people play – and impose on each other – in marriage. ('Admit it, there is someone else, isn't there?' reads one cartoon, with a picture of mum holding baby.) Brilliant book, warm and humane. Do read it.

The next thing you should do is to re-assess your marriage, get yourselves together. If you find it impossible to talk without arguing, you may like to go to your local Marriage Guidance Council and discuss those things that upset you with a neutral, trained person. This is often very helpful. Better to go while there is still a chance of patching things up rather than leave it until the family is on the verge of breaking up.

What you have to realize is that marriage is about friendship as well as love. It is about adjustment, making allowances, give and take and the constant renegotiation of the relationship. You've both moved on in the last five years. Now's the time to stop and think, to get your act together.

At the moment, he's in a play called *Pygmalion*. You're Eliza Doolittle; he's Professor Higgins and he's working on you. With luck and hard work, as he sees it, he could, despite the unpromising material, make you socially acceptable before too long. It's like trying to turn an apple into a banana, but he doesn't know that: he's out to make you something nearer to his fantasy woman.

It's not as bad as it sounds. We all have it — this type of conditional love: the 'I'll love if you're more tidy/less scatty/didn't wear jeans/didn't drop your H's' type. The 'I'd love you if you were someone else'. But you're not.

He's wrong to keep chipping away at you but, on the other hand, he's a good, loving father and he obviously isn't wholly at fault. What about you? You say later in your letter that you never put the keys back on the allocated hook. Why? Is it perhaps to annoy him? Is this nagging thing important to you? It's not fair on him to play the naughty child, or to do the 'I can't change, I'm ME, can't you see?' scenario. He's your partner, not a parent. You really do have to start relating to each other *as adults*.

At the moment you seem to be trapped in a child–adult mode of relating. He's doing all he can to treat you as a child. Why? Who is he comparing you with? You must tell him that these comparisons are unacceptable. Be an adult. Say to him, 'Cut it out.' Have a sense of humour about it and tell him to stop it.

He may be being bossy. I suspect that he's a man who feels a loss of confidence, is confused. The arrival of a first child can affect a man in this way. He may feel left out, rejected, worried that you'll fly away and find someone more interesting. He may feel that he's losing control within the family. He's not as strong as you want him to be.

You must stop playing the child and provoking him. Write, in indelible ink, PUT KEY ON RIGHT HOOK on the back of your hand. Come down from the clouds and make some adjustments yourself. Why do you want him to nag you? Is this a tactic to bring out his headmaster/strong man persona? Why do you need him to be like that?

Family isn't another word for plenty of abuse. You should treat each other as equals, as real people. You must do more things together, have some fun together. Find a babysitter and go out and relax *together*. Have some fun. If all the fun takes

118

place away from him, you'll grow apart as sure as God made little apples.

A good marriage has to be based on true friendship rather than the quicksands of romantic love. A good marriage is to do with growth, change and integrity. You have to be tough and honest with your partner (and with yourself). You have to sort out problems as they come along (not run away from them). You have to have commitment and say, 'This marriage is going to last.'

Being married to someone *is* taxing. It can be very rewarding if the couple grow together, work out common goals, aims and values they have in common. It may be that saving your marriage is not a major hurdle after all. All you both have to do is to stop messing about and actually say hello to each other. Then talk more, do more, grow more *as a family*.

Move towards friendship. Your man really is going to have to change. He's got to stop getting at you and begin to respect you as a person. You must develop the confidence to tell him how you want to be treated and to tell him to stop trying to turn you into his mother or some fantasy woman he has invented.

Your best bet is to take your man in your arms and say, 'You're precious and special. I love you.' (If you do.) Say, 'I'd never leave you.' (If you wouldn't.) Then say, 'From now on I want you to treat me as me and not as someone else/a child.' Go out and have fun together. You deserve it.

Being close to someone is to be able to be honest with them. Stop the silly role playing. Look at your situation now. Work out what you both want from your marriage. This is the time to re-assess.

With commitment, loyalty, hard work and a sense of humour, I think you'll win through. Everybody knows that marriage can be tough. Few people mention that it can also be great fun if you learn to look at each other as adults, and friends.

This invasion of psychological space and conditional love ('I'll love you if . . .') is often the result of what Eric Berne calls games (see *Games People Play*, by Eric Berne, M.D., Penguin Books) and I call Foxes and Rabbits. There is no harm in you being a fox and me being a rabbit if we both agree to it and both know what we're doing. It is when neither of us knows what is going on that the rabbit tends to come to grief. Each of us brings fantasies and

119

unfinished emotional business from the past. It is when these fantasies are acted out in the here and now that a great deal of confusion – and pain – can ensue.

According to transactional analysis theory, each of us has within us a parent, an adult and a child. In marriage this means that there are nine ways in which the two partners can relate at an unconscious level. As in the letter above, he may be the parent, she the child. In other relationships it may be the woman who is the parent, the man the child. In some marriages the relationship is that of child to child; in others, I'm glad to say, it is that of adult to adult.

In companionship marriage, by definition, the couple interact dynamically, and therefore more closely. This means more risk of unrealistic fantasies and destructive, unfinished business from the past being projected on to the partner. In fact, modern, dynamic schools of marital therapy base their approach on gaining insight into the psychological difficulties which the couple have brought to each other from their individual pasts.

In marriage, in my view, there should be an opportunity to express the inner child (the 4 year old which we all carry around within us), to have fun, to behave in a spontaneous, child-like way. It's hard being an adult (or a parent all the time). It is good to be dependent from time to time and it's pleasant to be looked after, to be spoilt. The main thing is that there should be negotiation about this, and justice: I'll spoil you, if you spoil me; we'll take turns at being the strong one, the child. It's when one partner acts like a small child *all* of the time that it's a strain on the partnership. This is particularly true when children come along.

In the early stages of marriage the main things to remember are:

1   *Your partner is a real person, not your father or your mother.* Some wives would do well to wear a sign, in the crucial first year, which reads, 'I am not your mummy.'
2   *Take your turn at being an adult and negotiate, honestly and openly, about roles – who does what and when.* To leave the major decision-making to one partner is storing up trouble for the future.
3   *Have some fun.* Marriage, like life, is no good if you don't have fun *some* of the time. Voltaire said that marriage is the cure for love. It doesn't have to be. If you *talk about* what you want from the relationship, trust each other (trust is vital in any relationship), give each other adequate space, then marriage *can* be very rewarding.

120

4   *If psychological games are spoiling your marriage, seek help*. These are to do with the past, not the here and now, and they can be very destructive. Do seek help from Marriage Guidance *before* your marriage is heading for the rocks. Many more marriages, in my view, could have been saved if help had been sought early enough.

5   *Respect your partner.* Good marriages, these days, contain respect and affection, treating the partnership as one in which equality and mutual support are paramount. No marriage will succeed without these elements of respect, equality — and justice.

I want to move on now to a further examination of roles and the necessity of growing alongside your partner. When one partner suddenly changes in a marriage, it may be very difficult for the other partner to cope. Consider the following example. It concerns a couple who, having spent ten years together in an instrumental, old-fashioned type of marriage, were suddenly faced with change, and with the challenge of a companionship-style of marriage in which their roles were drastically altered. For the man in the marriage it was a case of adapt or perish. He survived . . . just.

X, in the early years of her marriage, was the Earth Mother type. She bore two children, was the primary caretaker (as most women are). She actually liked the job. She cooked, washed and attended to the children's needs, springing forth with Elastoplast and fish fingers when and where required, taking them along to play group when they were older. Her husband, Y, went to his office in the morning. His meal was always ready for him when he returned in the evening.

It was when the second of the two children went to junior school that things changed. X bought herself a Renault, got herself a part-time job, joined a Beginners' Class in Italian and started to take an interest in local government. She went out several evenings a week.

Y was quite alarmed at the change in his wife. 'She used to be such a marvellous mother,' he told me. 'Now, she's out all the time and into every good cause you can think of.' She wasn't out all the time (and she was still a marvellous mum). It was simply that her change of image — her new identity, her new idea of who she was — had come very suddenly. Her partner had become used to her as a mum. Now he had to adjust to her as

121

a real person, an individual in her own right, with ideas of her own. Such sudden shifts *can* cause great stress in a marriage. There were many arguments between X and Y, sparked off by Y, simply because he couldn't come to terms with the change.

What is the solution to this sort of dilemma? If it's a woman who feels that her needs are now different, she must explain, quietly and without aggression, what those needs are. She must say, 'I now need a bigger canvas on which to paint the picture of my existence. I'm taking more space for myself. I now feel that I should do some things for *me* as well as the family. This is Me Time that I'm taking.' That's fair and within her rights. It's the way that it's explained that's crucial.

If a woman tells her partner about what is happening to her, the marriage has a much greater chance of survival. If she suddenly changes her pattern of behaviour, it can be very frightening to her man. The solution is to *talk*, openly and honestly. She should explain that mothering is about quality, not quantity, that it's not necessary to be with the children all of the time.

A mother with young children should be able to do some of the things she wants to do. She is an equal partner in the marriage and she shouldn't give up all her interests and community involvement. Besides, there is no output without input and a mother has more to give to her children when she is a real, fully rounded person. Some young mothers may want, and need, to take a part-time (or full-time) job. Why not, if it can be managed? Anything that gives a woman a break from routine, a chance to see the world beyond her own kitchen, staves off boredom and increases the quality of the contact between children and mother.

What women should avoid is colluding in an instrumental, 'Me Jane, You Tarzan' type of marriage and then, without warning, switching roles and insisting that, from now on, Tarzan makes his own tea. The thing as a man to avoid is to be the 'strong one' and suddenly change into the child, or be the 'master' (a self-appointed post) and suddenly find that the 'servants' are no longer obeying orders. Negotiation is based on a relationship, on information, and on options. In marriage, the relationship of the partners will change. The way to deal with it is to communicate needs and to work out, together, what the options are so that *both* partners may grow and have their own space.

It is worth adding that Y, after arguments, tears (on his part), threats (on his part) and much soul-searching accepted, eventually, the change that had taken place. What option did he have? It's very hard to stop human beings developing, reaching out to the community and to the wider world for affirmation and stimulation, if they're determined to do so. In accepting change, the marvellous thing was that he began a process of change and growth within himself. X and Y now have a companionship marriage. It took time but, then, anything worth achieving always does.

Communication is vital in a marriage — at each and every stage. Without open discussion of issues as they crop up, without an adult to adult discussion of needs and wants (and resentments), it's very hard for a marriage to weave its way through all the practical and emotional hazards that confront every couple. Every marriage that fails, fails through lack of communication. It isn't financial and sexual problems that destroy marriages; nor is it arguments over roles and psychological space. These are symptoms of that lack of communication which is at the heart of all marriage breakdowns. There are couples who live in a communication wilderness in which nothing vital — nothing about yearnings, love, feelings, hopes and desires — is ever discussed. In the following letter to 'On The Couch' my impression is one of an awfully lonely person, and of two people living together as strangers under the same roof. Here's the letter:

Does anyone know what they want from life or is that something only a few people get to find out?

I'm a confused 23 year old, married to a man of 28. I expected the normal things from a marriage — a nice house, car, kids, etc. — but now I think it would be better if I had these things on my own (though I'm not sure).

How will I know the grass is greener elsewhere? By the time I get there it could be too late! Is this the gamble people take with life and if it is how do I know which stakes to bet on? What helps one to decide?

I've been unfaithful and consider my lover important but not permanent. I've had no physical relationship with my husband for the past year. This is of my own choice. He's very good to me and loves me very much but I don't feel I can fulfil the commitments of my marriage.

123

I have never been on my own before and I feel a mixture of uncertainty and excitement. I realize that many young women of my age would envy me, with a lovely home, doting husband and a secure job, but for me it isn't enough. I don't know what the right thing to do is and I don't want to do anything that I will regret later. Can you advise me?

Here is part of my answer:

You *must* take steps to solve your dilemma. You could list the facts and the possible choices or courses of action. Then you can talk about your situation with trusted friends. I believe in the Talking Cure; not Freud's obsession with the past, but talking about the *present* situation, clarifying it in your mind. It does help.

Then you must *do* something. Tell your husband, quietly and seriously, how you feel. Ask him how he feels (his happiness is involved too). Go along together to Marriage Guidance Counselling (find the number in the telephone directory) and discuss if there is any chance of saving your marriage. When you've done all that it'll be time to choose, one way or another.

Don't hedge your bets. There are no medals for uncertainty. Get the best advice you can covering all aspects of your marriage and then make a decision. Life isn't a rehearsal for the show. This *is* the show and you have to start speaking *your* lines, singing *your* tune, getting *your* act together. Do it now. Respect yourself.

I would never advise anyone to stay in a totally bleak, loveless marriage. On the other hand, many marriages can be saved if there is commitment, and a willingness to stop travelling down different roads, be a little more open and honest, share a few more dreams, talk a little more to each other. Talk it out: talk, talk, talk. In marriage, jaw-jaw is always better than war-war. A large part of marriage is sympathy and empathy: seeing things from the partner's point of view. How can empathy be established if you don't talk about things together, especially about your feelings, and your dreams?

Marriage, these days, is under attack. There are those who say that it can't work, cynics who write on walls: Marriage Rots the Brain. There have always been cynics about marriage. One Frenchman claimed that a woman waits for the right man to come along, and in the meantime she gets married. George

Bernard Shaw wrote: 'Marriage is tolerable enough in its way, if you're easy going and don't expect too much from it. But it doesn't bear thinking about.'

I think we *have* to think about marriage; it is the pivotal institution within society. If there were a viable alternative to marriage, I am sure we would have found it by now. Communes, by and large, don't work; they don't provide sufficient security and privacy. People don't want to live alone; they want to face life as a couple. Most people who make that 'till death us do part' promise really mean it. So how can marriage be made to work and what should couples do if they don't want to join that one-third of marriages which are destined to fail?

In my view the main things to remember in marriage are:

1   *Start as you mean to go on.* Share, treat each other as equals, discuss who does what. If you collude in destructive games − or are a willing victim − you can't be surprised if you're taken advantage of. If you wait on your man hand and foot when you're first married, you're storing up trouble for later on. Have a roster of jobs, a weekly conference. Keep it practical − and equal.

2   *Give each other space.* No couple should live in close proximity 24 hours a day; that's not intimacy, that's claustrophobia. Let him have a night out. Make sure you have one too. Do things together and separately and you'll appreciate each other more.

3   *Don't get used to dull routines, and end up taking each other for granted.* Do something different, something exciting, from time to time. It's up to you whether you keep the romance alive in your marriage. *Insist* on little adventures together even if it's only making love in the kitchen with you in your hair rollers or him wearing wellington boots, or both.

4   *Reward each other.* What keeps marriages alive is not perfect sex, but little shows of affection: a kiss, a hug, a cuddle. These are all powerful rewards, as is praise. Don't nag: talk it out.

5   *Share the bad as well as the good.* Disabuse your man of the quaint notion that changing a baby's nappy is woman's work. Leave him with the children for a weekend. There's no better way of convincing a man that looking after children all day is an incredibly tiring task.

6 *Accept change.* Be flexible in your roles, and in what you want from your relationship. It will alter as the marriage progresses, but do say what you want and need. Treat your partner not as a parent or a child, but as an adult and, even more vital, a friend. Talk about your worries, fears, hopes, little moments of triumph. That's what friends do.

7 *Be a person as well as a mother (or father).* Don't be a martyr. Don't sacrifice your life to the family. This will make everybody within reach feel guilty and it will do nothing for your own personal growth or development. Take an interest in community affairs; have friends outside of the marriage. Marriage isn't a prison; it's a safe base from which to live your life.

8 *Be realistic about marriage.* There is no 'ideal marriage'. There is only the marriage that you make for yourself. Say: 'I want this.' Discuss it with your partner and make sure you get some of what you want. Don't expect marriage to supply all your social, intellectual and emotional needs. It was never meant to do that. You can fulfil yourself if you get out, make friends and do things with and for others in the community.

9 *Expect rows, arguments, fights.* Every marriage has some. Keep a sense of humour about it, talk it out and, if necessary, see a counsellor. With common sense, plenty of honest discussion (and perhaps a little help from a neutral, professional counsellor) many a marriage could be saved. It's a great achievement to stay married. It's the *only* way you get to know the end of the story.

10 *Take turns to spoil each other.* Treat each other as sentient, thinking human beings, and treat your spouse no worse than you would treat your best friend. Love is important to marriage; friendship is even more important.

Why is marriage so popular? It is because people do need something to believe in, do need a commitment, something to work at that isn't transient, here today and gone tomorrow. It is because living with someone you like is better than living alone; sharing adventures, sharing the journey of life is better than having those adventures or travelling alone. Marriage these days is a formidable task. It is because each couple must decide between themselves what sort of marriage they want. It is a formidable task, but a very exciting one. Most people do want their marriages to last, have the commitment to stay around long enough to find out the end of the story.

Chapter 10
The family

Somewhere, over the rainbow, there is the 'perfect family': mum, dad, the children – one of each – never a cross word spoken. Everything in the house works perfectly; nobody ever argues; the wife has the most beautifully smooth hands. This little family is very like the ones in the television advertisements. They live in a house where they worry about small grease stains on the kitchen floor. This makes you feel guilty – in *your* house it is just as well to wipe your feet on going out rather than on coming in.

I've never met a perfect family. The ones I know are all slightly odd. They have funny ways of doing things, funny habits. Tolstoy said that all happy families resemble each other, but every unhappy family is unhappy in its own way. I've never found this to be true. Every family is different. What works in one may not work in another. One happy family runs the show very much like the Royal Marines; strangely, they're happy. Another family has a very permissive, go-as-you-please atmosphere; that works too. However you run your family, I'm for it, providing it works for everybody concerned.

To be absolutely honest, I'm not sure what a family is these days. I was born in an extended family, with lots of relatives living in the same place. There was an extensive network of kith and kin, myriad aunts and uncles, cousins – dozens of them – and vaguely related people all around. Life pulsated out, through the house, the road, the community. Few of us live in that kind of family any more.

Most of us live in nuclear families, just parents and children, living away from our relatives: that ready-made support system. Families are smaller. You may or may not know your neighbours. The nuclear family can become very isolated, claustrophobic, explosive when it isn't part of a supportive network, when it doesn't reach out to the community.

Cynics will tell you that a family is just a means of controlling

128

people. It's a handy, mobile unit. It gobbles up consumer goods – televisions, fridge-freezers, food – and doesn't cause too much trouble (watching, as it does, up to six hours of television per day). It's hard to be a rebel with a mortgage hanging around your neck. Families are to do with consumerism, and control.

Perhaps. I consider the family to be the basic unit of society. It's the best thing we've thought up so far to rear children and prepare them for life. By and large, it works better than kibbutzim in Israel (see Bruno Bettelheim's *The Children of the Dream*, Thames & Hudson), or communes in the USSR. They've been tried and found wanting – in that close, loving, tender care that children need. The family is the source of our greatest joys and our greatest woes. We are stuck with it. The aim has to be to make it work.

The family, as a basic unit, doesn't have to be parents plus children, living in a semi-detached house. Some people live in hippy communes, in tepees. Others live in squats. In that typical semi, there may be a single parent living with the children, or mum with a new partner, living with three of hers and two of his. There may be two women, living together, rearing the children of previous marriages. The family, these days, is a moveable feast. It can include new members, dispense with others, assume a new shape.

Maybe a family is just a group of people who gather round the hearth together, sharing the same hopes and the same dreams. Maybe the family we all ought to be concentrating on these days is one called the human race. Nowadays we live in a global village and what one nation does affects the rest of us. Perhaps we're moving, slowly, towards a Family of Man (and Woman).

Be that as it may. What I'm going to do is to assume that you live in a nuclear family of parent(s) plus child(ren) and you want to know how to make it work. You'll have had little preparation for the responsibilities of parenthood and you are finding that bringing up children is a very demanding job indeed. When you have a child, you're never the same again. You move from being an adult to being a parent. It's a life-time's task.

Let's have a look at the preparation for parenthood. If you are a mother, you may have been told, at school, how to bath a baby. You may have had lessons in housecraft, cooking, homecare. What you will not have been told is how you will feel as a mother; you will have been told very little about the emotional impact of parenthood.

129

You will not have been told that you may not feel an immediate overwhelming love for the baby, that you may feel tired, depressed, inadequate, terrified. You will not have been told that *all* young mothers feel washed out at times, exhausted, done in. You will not have been told about your partner's possible reactions to the new baby. You may know about baby foods, but you will almost certainly be thrown in at the deep end as far as your feelings are concerned.

As a father, you will have received even less preparation for parenthood. You may not know what fathers do (the only job description you have is what *your* father did, which may or may not work in your new family). You may find yourself mystified by family life – and shocked by the sheer hard graft. Perhaps you will go off to 'work' in the morning with a sigh of relief and tell your mates or colleagues, 'Bringing up children is woman's work.' You may read one of the books available now which tells you what fathering involves (such as Tony Bradman's *The Essential Father*, Unwin), or you may hope you can just cruise along, taking the good bits from the family and leaving the really hard work to your wife.

Both mothers and fathers have fantasies about 'the family'; mother may think that she'll be a Super Mum, kind and gentle, never tired or fed up; her children will always do the right things – sleep at night, eat heartily, never cry; dad may fantasize that his role is to pat the children on the head at night before they go to bed, rather like the Colonel of the Regiment reviewing the troops. Both mum and dad will have seen ideal families on television (and will have their own versions of that over the rainbow family). The reality of family life may come as a great shock to them both.

I speak from experience. Imagine the scene. *Time*: twenty-odd years ago. *Place*: a small house on a large estate. Me, a young father, left with baby and bottle, told to feed babe at 11 am. The designated hour arrives. Warms milk, holds bottle in various positions. Loud screams from baby. Call through window to neighbour. She enters house. 'Give her to me,' she says. Takes hold of baby and bottle. Baby feeds immediately. I stand aside, somewhat ashamedly, and watch.

How many men, these days, take a share in the child-minding and know what to do with babies/young children? Shouldn't parenthood be a core curriculum subject in every secondary school – for both boys and girls? Fathers vary a great deal nowadays. Many care and share; many don't. Some haven't a clue as to what fathering is about, others adopt the Louis XIV stance towards the rest of the family. No wonder many women claim that the central issue in a modern family is: *who minds the children*?

To create a happy family is as great an achievement as painting the *Mona Lisa*. To make a modern family *work*, you need flexibility of roles, caring and sharing (of the grotty as well as the happy times). You need love, devotion, commitment. You have to be able to cope with change. You adapt or perish. Then, you have to have a large measure of unselfishness. Rearing a family is no easy task. Consider the following two scenarios.

1 *Decisions*. He is a very able professional man. She is a teacher (who works part-time) with two children, both under five. He is offered a job in a different part of the country, one that is a real opportunity to use his undoubted talents. She, with her job, network of friends and her two little girls who are very happy where they are, doesn't want to move. She hates the thought of moving to a northern county, where she knows no one and where she, and the children, will have to start building up those networks of friendship all over again.

The outcome? She went. 'The family has to stick together,' she says. Quite right. *Question: will a time ever come when a woman's needs are given priority?*

2 *Change.* He had been a hero, Captain Marvellous, in the family. If a query arose about something, she would say to the children, 'Ask your father.' If there were guests for dinner, she'd say, 'John says the wine is superb.' John, her husband, was a man whose role within the family was that of benevolent dictator. Then, at 42, John lost his job and became very depressed. She could rely on him for his salary − and to make the decisions − no longer. She had to assume the role of leader. *Question: what happens within a family when radical changes take place and when the members of the family have to assume new roles?*

A family is an organic thing: it grows and changes, goes through good times − and through bad times. At each stage of the family each member of the group will have different needs and wants. Each family goes through a constant process of change and re-evaluation. If the family provides sufficient rewards for all of its

131

members it will last; if there are no rewards – just hard work with little emotional support and no *fun* for one of the partners – the family may be in danger. How do we make sure that the family provides a safe base – and sufficient rewards – for each of its members?

My advice to young wives is *to start as you mean to go on*. If it is a companionship marriage you have embarked on then, family-wise, you'll be keen on caring and sharing. Enjoy the pregnancy together, don't let your man treat you as his mother/maid/whore. Remember, you are friends and friends should share the good times and the bad. Make sure he is a participatory dad, and that includes lots of emotional support and practical help for you during pregnancy. Always refer to 'our baby'.

When your baby comes alone, take turns to get up in the night to see if the baby's still there. Your partner may or may not have been present at the birth, but whether he was or not, he too needs to bond with the baby. Let him have a turn at holding the baby, feeding it, changing its nappy. Then, leave him with the babe whilst you go and have a cup of coffee with a neighbour or have your hair done. If he doesn't learn at this stage, when will he?

Mum may be depressed after the birth of the baby. This is where a dad can help by being patient and understanding, affectionate and supportive. He can tell his wife that her feelings are nothing to be ashamed of and that she doesn't have to cope alone: that the family doctor can help by listening, by reassurance – or by supplying medication, if necessary, to tide her over the bad patch.

Dad may be jealous of the new baby. If, before the arrival of the baby, he has been acting out some Louis XIV fantasy, he will be less than pleased at his dethronement. Even good, caring and sharing dads can feel some resentment – or confusion – that they are no longer the centre of their wives' attention. This is why mum needs to be sensitive, to give her partner a share in the baby, to give him responsibility, and to ask him about his feelings. Talk it out; be loving to each other; give your man some tender loving care at this time. Mothers, too, can be jealous of the affection that a father can lavish on the new baby. Solution? Be extra specially affectionate towards each other at this time, and open and honest about your feelings. What is marriage without an honest expression of what is going on inside you?

132

The aim with children is to move from love towards friendship (and to learn to love 'em and leave 'em be). This is the love stage. Give the baby lots of it: lots of cuddles, holding, contact comfort (from both mum and dad). Babies need lots of cuddles. So do adults. Whilst you're loving the baby (and the more loving the better), don't forget to take time off to cuddle each other.

Work out a routine, decide who does what, and stick to it. A new baby needn't disrupt your life. Buy a baby buggy/baby carrier. Don't suddenly become totally home-centred and give up your social contacts. Every family exists within a context of community support. If there is not one already, start up a baby-sitting group so you can go out when you want to. Enjoy your life. Having a child doesn't mean becoming a hermit. What counts, with mothering *and* fathering, is *quality* not quantity. You don't have to be with the baby 24 hours a day to be a good mum (or dad).

If you need to work, find a good child-minder (make a few enquiries from your friends or Social Services) and *don't* feel guilty about leaving your baby in her care. What the baby wants is you, at your best, a giving mother, and there is no output without input. How can you give to your baby if you don't get any outside stimulation yourself? Don't worry if you need to go out to work so long as, when you are with your baby, you *do* give and both enjoy each others' company.

Look for — or create — that support network in the community. If there isn't a mums' Cuppa Club or a Mother and Toddler group in your neighbourhood, why not start one? Find out what crèche and nursery facilities there are (again, Social Services will tell you, look them up in the telephone directory). Find out what is happening in the way of community support and join in. The family's a safe base, not a prison; it's a platform from which to spring to enjoy the world: it was never meant to supply all our needs — emotional, intellectual or social.

If you're a woman, leave the infant in your partner's care whilst you go off for a day (or even a weekend). There's no finer way I know of impressing upon a man how much hard work — and, sometimes, fun — there is involved in looking after children. A little absence makes the heart grow fonder and what applies to dads applies to mums. So, do have a break from time to time. With motherhood there are no medals for being a martyr.

133

Caring and sharing is your motto. You may, as mum, have the responsibility for the day care of the infant. Probably, it's you that will take the child to playgroup, find other mums to visit so that the children can play together. This doesn't mean, though, that your man does nothing. In the evening he can cuddle, read to, play with the children. He can mind them if you want to go out in the evening or you can find a baby-sitter and go out together. Dads are vital in a family. At least they can be another friendly, participating adult to have around the place. At most, they can really share in, and have all the fun that goes with, the magic of young children.

Dads are important. The father is a girl's first model of 'a man'. How her father relates to her will affect, in some way, her future relationships and trust of men. Boys, too, need an adequate father-figure if they are to grow into men. A happy son–father relationship can be a warm overcoat to protect a child from the chill winds of life; a happy daughter–father relationship can be one of the most rewarding – indeed, beautiful – experiences in life.

What about single-parent mothers, those families where there is no father? If you are a single-parent mum you may worry about your child not having a father-figure to whom he can relate. You should inform the playgroup, nursery or school of the family situation and perhaps one of the men helpers or teachers could build up a relationship with your child. Boys can be encouraged to join the cubs, scouts (or some sports club) where they will meet suitable father-substitutes. Girls, too, at youth clubs and other organizations can build up a good relationship with a man who will act as a father-figure. The home may not have a father, but the community has plenty of father-figures. When mother and children take up interests that bring them in contact with adults of both sexes, it gives the children a chance to relate to men, and the chance to identify with a kind, caring and worthwhile man. There are such men in the world, and in your local community.

Life isn't only about families – life is about people. The purpose of the family is to rear and protect children, and to pass on the culture into which they are born. However, adults – and children – have a life outside of the family. The family can't supply all our wants and needs. To be really fully developed individuals we must all learn to: (a) have realistic expectations of family life; (b) live some of our lives outside, out there, in the

134

community where we can get the stimulation we need to make us more able and willing to cope with family demands.

These realistic expectations should also be applied to the 'good' mother. Children don't need Florence Nightingale (or Mary Poppins) as a mum. What they need is a mum who loves them and does what she can for them. The 'perfect' mother doesn't exist. What children need is a 'good enough' mum. The same thing applies to dads. Children don't want Sigmund Freud as a dad, they just want some time and attention from their own dad (or a suitable father-figure). There are no perfect families — only 'good enough' ones.

As a good enough parent your aim should be, in the words of Dr Winnicott, to make an 'active adaptation to the child's needs, starting off with complete devotion and then adapting less and less to the wishes of the infant as time goes on'. See *Playing and Reality*, by D. W. Winnicott, Penguin Books.) This is what Freud calls moving away from the Pleasure Principle towards the Reality Principle. It's what I call common sense. Children have needs (love, security; affection, adventure, stimulation), but so do parents. The good enough parent and child learn to love each other more when they have little breaks from each other.

The implications of looking at families in this way are enormous. You'll spoil your children sometimes, you'll shout at them when you're tired, this is normal. (Remember, the 'ideal' family is a myth.) The infant learns to adapt to the mother's failure (Winnicott's word) to supply all his/her needs. The mother comes to realize that she has needs of her own *and* that it is acceptable to have these needs. *Children have needs, but so do parents.* Often, they're the same needs.

Children need praise, prestige, responsibility (so do mums and dads). They need tender, loving care (so do adults). They need stimulation, adventure, affection, a chance to prove themselves (ditto). There is nothing mysterious about the needs of children. They are the basic needs of *all* human beings.

Here are ten basic rules for dealing with children. They apply to children of any age, to young children as well as teenagers. As children grow older, you will give them more responsibility, more space to make their own decisions, more room to make their own mistakes. *The rules, however, will stay the same.* Here they are:

1 *Tell your children you love them.* There will be times when you do not like what they do; but don't forget, from time to time, to say, 'I love you.' Those words count (just as they do with adults).

2 *Express affection.* A hug and a cuddle, plus a word of praise, is worth a shilling an ounce. What's the use of loving them if you never show it? Don't behave as though cuddles (or an arm around the shoulder) were gold sovereigns. Dispense affection liberally; it costs nothing.

3 *Treat children courteously.* They are not monsters after all. If you treat them like creatures from Mars, they'll behave that way. Act as though you expect them to do as you ask, then they will. Respect them and they will respect you.

4 *In times of annoyance, be a 'good enough' mum (or dad) not a 'make-it-worse' mum (or dad).* Be brisk; say, 'I don't like that' or 'Don't do that', with feeling. Then, forget it. I once heard a mother say to a little girl in a supermarket, 'If you do that again, I'll break every bone in your body.' The little girl was about 3 years old and had touched a can of beans. Just the word 'Don't' should be enough (accompanied by one of your looks).

5 *Say no sometimes, however old they are.* When you say it, mean it. Practise saying no in the mirror before you ever become a parent. It's a *very* useful word.

6 *Have some rules.* The fewer the better, but no human group can exist without any rules. Once you have established them, stick to them and make sure everybody knows why those rules apply.

7 *Praise your children, even your teenagers.* Human beings respond to praise much more than to criticism. I do; you do; they do. Thank them when they've done something helpful: don't just tell them off when they've done something awful.

8 *Give them responsibility.* Do this from an early age. Don't do everything for them. (What kind of preparation for life is that?) As teenagers, let them have an allowance to buy their own clothes, let them help with the meals and in the house. In my own family we had 'A Day of Hell' in which each member of the family – on his or her day – cooked breakfast and the evening meal (and washed the dishes and tidied the house). It quickly cured them of the notion that the house was a hotel in which they were non-paying guests.

Even my youngest daughter insisted on doing her day. She was then, as I remember, about 9. Her meals were simple, but palatable. Children like responsibility. Why not give them some?

9 *Give them prestige.* 'Mark's good at making omelettes.' 'Jane's marvellous with anything mechanical.' Develop a special interest, a special talent in each child, give each child a definite place in the car park of the family. Don't compare. Give each child his/her due as a unique human being.

10 *Listen to your children (especially your teenagers).* You will learn a lot from them. There are parents who *never* listen and this is very annoying to children of any age (just as it is annoying to an adult who says something important and isn't listened to). Talking is important but listening is even more vital. How can you know what they're feeling if you don't say, 'Tell me about it?' Then listen, carefully, and with respect.

As your children get older, community involvement will become as important to them as it is to you. Cubs and brownies, clubs and hobbies, sport and outdoor activities all enhance individual skill and provide an opportunity to meet a range of people outside of the family. Sometimes you will feel that your job as parent is nothing more than being a taxi-driver. Just remember they need those interests, those outside contacts. One new club joined, one new interest (anything from ice-skating to swimming from tap-dancing to roller-skating) is worth hours of psychoanalysis or a discussion on the problem of living together with children.

It is when their children become teenagers that many parents come to feel that they are total failures as parents. What happened to those lovely children they once knew? Who are these ETs (Enormous Teenagers) who have suddenly appeared in the home? Why are they always using the telephone, making such a row, going into a sulk, refusing to tidy their bedrooms. Why does your once-adored son talk like a caveman? Why does your erstwhile flaxen-haired daughter look like an Indian brave? You're not alone; you simply have teenagers.

A friend of mine, a bachelor, once asked me what it was like having teenage children. I told him: it's like lying in bed, unable to sleep, when your daughter's out late (or, worse, having learned to drive, out in the car). It's worrying yourself sick over 'unsuitable' (ie, for you) friends or wondering whether your son has a speech defect because all he seems to have said for the past two years is 'Yah' or 'Nah'. (Or 'Awrigh' — all right — when asked, by you, 'What was school like today?) When you have teenagers, it's a time for renegotiation (not forgetting those rules) and a time to try to move towards mutual respect, and friendship. It is not easy.

Let me provide two examples from my own experience as a parent of teenagers. *Place*: our house. *Time*: Six years ago. An Enormous Teenager knocks at the front door. Jeeves-like, I go to answer. 'Ugh, ugh, ugh,' says the ET. On hearing the voice, my son rushes downstairs. Plaster falls from the hall ceiling. 'Ugh,' the two teenagers greet each other with casual enthusiasm: 'Yah, nah, ugh, ugh, ugh.' My wife and I looked at each other over dinner that evening. 'Where did we go wrong?' I asked. 'Have you ruled out deafness?' asked my wife. There was no deafness. There was only that strange, monosyllabic way teenagers have of talking to each other.

Example Two: one morning at 8 am I left our Dorset home for London. My eldest daughter was sitting on the front door step, chatting to a friend on the phone. When I returned at 7 pm, she was still there. My God, I thought, the phone bill. Luckily, it was a different friend. My daughter has friends all over the country and used to run what appeared to be a nationwide, free, agony aunt service.

Your teenagers may be too talkative or silent or untidy. They may get on your nerves, playing pop music all the time. Perhaps they treat the house like a hotel, with you as the janitor/cook. How do you live with teenagers in peace and harmony? Let's look at some of the possibilities.

Negotiation: discuss who does what, and when. Have lists and rosters pinned up so that everyone knows the form. Give them definite responsibilities. If they are untidy, encourage them to invite friends around to the home. This is the best way I know to make them tidy up.

Homework: encourage them to get into a routine for doing it. If you have any doubts about the homework, ask the school's advice. When exam time comes along (and they disappear upstairs white-faced), be encouraging and supportive. Buy them a copy of *Learn How to Study* by Derek Rowntree so that they can develop effective study and revision habits. Then leave them to get on with it. Never moan. Be positive in what you have to say.

Praise: everybody needs PPR (praise; prestige; responsibility), but especially teenagers. Don't say things like, 'You're not going out looking like that are you?' Why do you think he/she has taken three hours to get ready? Don't hark on things that annoy you. Discuss them openly and do something about them, just as friends would.

Prestige: give them a chance to develop special interests, look out for any special talents and help them to develop them. Every human being is a genius; some have a genius for playing the piano; others have a genius for being kind and loving. Every teenager has his/her own worth.

Responsibility: give them a clothes allowance. Go with them (if they want you to) when they choose their clothes. Chat about sex with them over the kitchen sink. (Why not? Tell them how shy you were when you were a teenager.) Be open and honest and *trust them* with their friends (what else can you do?). Make them responsible for getting home after an evening out. If it worries you, make sure they know the time of the last bus. Let them cook the Sunday meal, invite friends to dinner, do the week's shopping. If a family is caring and sharing, then treat teenagers as sensible, sentient beings who want to make a contribution. Don't patronize them. And don't be afraid to say no (perhaps to that motor-bike; that week in a tent, at 13, with a mixed sex group), but say *why*. Give your reasons. If they ask you about drugs, say, 'Just say no.' If they ask you about sex, say, 'It's dangerous.' Give your views. Be brisk, crisp and factual and don't forget to listen when they tell you their views. Treat them with courtesy and concern and give them lots of responsibility. This is the way to make the generation gap (which is necessary to maintain *some* space) bearable, even enjoyable.

What happens if, while you are concentrating on the rearing of the children, the relationship between you and your spouse is becoming less and less rewarding? What can parents do to ensure that the home isn't completely child-centred and that they, as adults, have a good, rewarding relationship with each other? After all, *this* relationship is the foundation on which the family rests. Spouses can grow and change together – or they can grow apart. A relationship, like a plant, has to be nurtured. What happens when it becomes stale, flat and neglected? Consider the following marriage. The letter is one from 'On The Couch'.

139

I'm in a relationship that is standing still, becoming dull and boring. I'm trying desperately to put some life into it but I have lost that love and respect I once had for my husband. I need a fuller life, more fulfilment and a stimulating man who is going to shower me with roses and take initiatives.

I've been married 12 years, have two lovely children and a dog. They need me, my husband dotes on me but doesn't know how to cope with me. He wants a quiet life, with a loving wife and no disruption. I'd love to be far away: to be me.

I have a part-time job but no inner peace, no contentment. I'm 38 and feel that − sooner or later − I will have to go, but we have no money for two homes, etc. What about my responsibilities and commitments? Do they matter? Can I just leave and start life over again?

I'm wearing myself out, have lost a lot of weight and I wonder where it will end. Does one have to destroy oneself like this? I could not bear the children to be hurt but how I long to love someone who I can talk to, have fun with and have a one-to-one relationship.

Should I stop expecting more than I am getting? Am I being self-centred and cruel? Will one be a better person for putting one's loved ones first? The questions go round and round in my head. One day I am staying, the next going. Please help.

What has happened in this marriage? It reminds me of the empty nest syndrome (although this nest isn't yet empty) in which, the children gone, the partners may look at each other and find that they don't know each other any more. They have to start getting to know each other again − renegotiating their relationship, doing things together and − now they have more time and, hopefully more money − having little adventures together, having fun. They do this or remain strangers to each other. (There is a rise in the incidence of divorce at this 'empty nest' stage of a marriage. Most of these divorces spring from the results of a relationship that has been neglected, allowed to whither, whilst the task of raising a family has been going on.) It is vital for parents to maintain their relationship, have some fun together, *throughout the marriage*.

Consider Y's letter. She and her husband appear to have an imbalance in their union. He dotes on her; she'd like to be elsewhere. She has an obligation to herself to lead a fulfilled life;

she has her duty towards the children; she has obligations towards her husband. Should she leave home, children and husband and look for her happiness elsewhere?

Before she does, she should say hello to her man, talk to him as adult to adult, and *tell him what she wants and needs*. The lump in her custard is boredom. Couldn't she ask her man to look after the children while she fulfils some of her needs? Could she take responsibility for herself and get a full-time job, start up a business, read for a degree, widen her horizons and gain the space she needs – or is her marriage doomed to fail?

What Y mustn't do is to ask her man what he thinks of her plans for self-realization; that is rather like asking a lamp-post what it thinks of dogs or asking a turkey how it feels about Christmas. She should state, clearly, quietly, what she wants to do, what she is going to do, and take active steps towards achieving the intellectual and social stimulation she so obviously needs. It is then, when she has gained some of the rewards that she needs, that she should review her marriage, and decide whether to go. She has colluded in allowing her husband to dote on her as the 'good mother'. Now he must adapt to her current needs. He'll grow as well, perhaps: reach out for new patterns, a new, less dependent way, new ideas or new roles. He could change as well, if she said what she wanted from him. He'll change, or he'll lose her.

This is what a family is about: growing up together, in friendship. It is about communication, love, being open about your wants, doubts and fears. There is no boss in a family (there's no boss between friends). In a family, nothing need be pre-determined. Everything is open to discussion and negotiation. This is a part of all viable groups. Y should give her husband a chance to be the sort of man she wants. She should be the sort of woman she wants to be. Then, she can make her choices. The family is about choices, and change.

This social context of the family has changed (that's why we all need to be community orientated, and not expect all our rewards in – and from – the family group). Our expectations with regard to the family, whether we are male or female (but especially if we're female), are higher. We all want more: whether it be consumer durables, emotional and sexual satisfaction, intimacy (feeling close to somebody), companionship, love and happiness. How do we get it?

Certain things have to be remembered if a marriage is to be

141

successful. For example, what is so tiring about your children is being with them. *all the time.* That's why caring and sharing is vital and why the husband who won't lift a finger is as of out of fashion as the dinosaur (or should be). This is why friends and all those community supports – playgroups, holiday play schemes, youth clubs – are vital to mothers (and fathers).

Mothers should remember that there is no universal mothering instinct. It you don't get any satisfaction out of mothering, you may have to face up to the fact that your infant would be better off with a registered child-minder, while you go out to office, factory or wherever you find the financial and emotional rewards you need. Don't feel guilty about it. You'll be a better mother for it. You may have to work. Again, better to be a giving, interested mum when you are with your child all the time.

Fathers should remember that their role isn't an optional extra in the modern family. It is absolutely vital. A man has to be a friend and companion to his wife if the modern family is going to work. He cannot take a spectator role. It simply gets too tough if the man doesn't do his bit, is more ornament than friend, imagines that the Tarzan/Jane model of a close relationship will work. You may not be the best father in the world (who is?), but as long as you muck in, do your bit, participate and help with the children (and the chores) at least you'll be joining that growing band of men who really do enjoy marriage, and the magic of children. They have learned to share: there *are* many rewards and it's a much more interesting and enjoyable role than spectator. Attitude is all. If your attitude is 'All this children stuff has nothing to do with me', you are going to end up terribly lonely.

The non-participating father – that dinosaur, Andy Capp, Old Jolyon Forsyte – will end up wandering about, lonely and isolated, *with nothing relevant to say*: about life, about love, about the family, about children. Macho Man's views are doomed to extinction. Why? They don't count because they don't work – not these days, not in a modern marriage.

Partnership and equality is the answer. Treating our partner as a real person (not your mother, or a maid, or a whore). Having justice in the home so that what happens inside the home is fair to *both* partners, that is modern marriage. There is no other way.

If you want your family to stay together, you should:

1 *Sort things out before you start a family.* If you gave up your job to have children, would you have to ask him for money for clothes? If he gave up his job to look after the family – or was unemployed – how would you feel as the breadwinner? Negotiate all this in advance.

2 *Set an allowance for the partner who stays at home.* This should be a proportion of all income. Don't think in terms of handouts. Looking after children *is* work and part of a mutual arrangement. You don't need a written contract, but clarify all this in your minds before you start on your family.

3 *Insist on fulfilling some of your own needs.* Don't be a martyr. Don't devote your life to your children and/or to your partner. Continue to grow as a person yourself, keep in touch with Out There, the community. Otherwise, when your children are teenagers they won't have, in you, a viable person as a friend. When your children leave home you'll want to live your own life again, so make sure you attend to some of *your* social/intellectual needs while you are bringing them up.

4 *Don't be possessive about the children.* It's up to you to get your partner to take an active role, to join in. It may take longer if he helps, but it's better that way. Get the show on the road but make sure it's a joint production.

5 *Regard your family as a film, rather than a series of snapshots.* A family is a changing scenario with lots of twists and turns in the plot. So, discuss the plot as you go along; make it a joint script. Don't you be the producer, with him as director. It will only have a happy ending if you both direct, if you both have a say in family issues as you go along.

6 *Speak out about your grievances.* Don't store them up and explode weeks/years later. Talk them out, discuss them, as they occur. This way, you have a much better chance of solving them.

7 *If your family is in trouble, get help.* These days, there is no stigma attached to going along to your GP and asking him to refer you to the child guidance clinic for advice and/or family therapy. Better that than to try to cope alone with a problem. If your relationship with your partner is in difficulties, go along to Marriage Guidance and try to sort it out in good time. (If you have problems with sex, there

143

are trained sex counsellors available who can help you.)
Marriages do break up because the partners sought help too
late (or didn't seek help at all).

8   *Constantly re-assess.* If something doesn't work for you,
why not change it? What worked when the children were
young, may not work when they are teenagers. Be flexible
with regard to roles and responsibilities. The family which
is flexible and adaptable has a much better chance of
providing those personal/emotional rewards which every
family needs to survive.

9   *Say what you want, and need.* Why not? You are entitled.
It's what they don't know that harms children — or what
they're unsure of. So don't have any 'hidden agenda' in the
family, stored up grievances, things which are on your mind
but which you never express. Children have very sensitive
emotional antennae, so bring your problems out into the
open where everybody can have a say, and at least know
how you feel.

10 *Have fun, sometimes.* Life is no good if you never have any
fun. A family is an awful place to be if people never relax,
act kindly towards each other and — from time to time —
simply have fun. In a family love is important, but so is
friendship, and good friends have fun together. See your
family as real friends, pals, buddies and you'll be well on
your way to treating them as they — the rest of the family
— ought to be treated.

Chapter 11
Work and play

You meet someone new and start a conversation. Sooner or later that person asks you, 'What do you do?' You say what you do (ie, your job) and the other person has an immediate idea of your class, income and life-style.

Sometimes, your answer may affect the way in which the person talks to you, reacts to you. I met a woman at a party recently. She told me, without my asking her, that she was a housewife and mother and we immediately started talking about disposable nappies, babies and the price of baby clothes. Later, she mentioned she was a qualified doctor. The conversation changed. 'What do you think about food additives and hyperactivity in children?' I asked her. We started chatting about the possible effects of lead pollution on children's behaviour. Despite myself (and I'm one of those people who believe that what you do is *not* what you are), my attitude towards the woman changed. Being a doctor had altered her identity. She was no longer 'just a mum', but a person with a job which has high status in most societies.

I try to avoid asking people what they do. (The answer to the question should be, 'When?') People ask me, though. When I tell them I'm a psychologist they ask me, 'Can you read my mind?' (The answer to that is: 'What makes you think I'd want to?') All I want to assert is that people *are* interested in what other people do. Work is a large part of our identity.

Work is terribly important to all of us. It gives us an identity, status, a sense of belonging, a role in society. It gives us the opportunity to belong to a group, to make new friends and acquaintances. It isn't only a doorway to social contacts, to the community, also it provides us with a daily programme of activity, a reason for getting up in the morning. It often gives us dignity, imposes a discipline on our lives and, last but not least, provides us with money.

145

Work is not solely about money. If it was, rich people wouldn't work. Those with independent means wouldn't become members of parliament, industrial tycoons, merchant bankers. They don't simply work because it is involving, interesting: it also provides all those other things I've mentioned.

I once met a man who had been left half a million pounds by a maiden aunt. He was a prep school teacher. 'I like teaching,' he told me. He could have invested the money, gone to live in Bermuda, Majorca, sat around all day doing nothing. But after a few weeks/months/years, this usually loses its appeal. Most people seem to *need* to work.

There are rich people who do not work, but money – and tradition – enables these people to handle the problem of ideleness much more effectively. They have a programme of leisure: they go to their clubs, visit their stables, go to certain summer resorts (and the 'in' ski resorts in winter). They hunt, fish and shoot at the appropriate seasons. This is a special group. Time is no problem for them: they have the money to fill that time with what, for them, is meaningful activity.

The majority of unemployed people aren't rich. Most of them have time for everything and money for nothing. It is not so easy to cope with leisure when you are hard up. It is even worse to cope with when you have been brought up on a Calvinist work ethic in which God looks favourably on those who work, whilst the devil finds work for idle hands to do. Many of us *do* feel guilty if we don't work. We feel a sense of shame, of failure. Work is very closely bound up with self-respect. To be out of work *can* rob us of our self-esteem.

Many people will tell you how they felt when they first lost their job. Initially there is the sense of shock, followed by a spell of actively hunting for a job during which the person remains fairly optimistic. Then, having failed to find a job, the man or woman becomes pessimistic and anxious. Then, lastly, a fatalism – the fatalism of hopelessness sets in and the individual succumbs to the stigma and shame of unemployment.

Quite a few young people, teenagers – sincere, bright, energetic and willing to work – may have never had a proper job. Many of them feel depressed and suffer from 'dole-sickness' – a mixture of shame, lethargy and hopelessness. Twenty years ago all of them would have found work. Now, some of them lay in bed until 1 pm; some watch television for much of the day, just to pass the time. It's not easy to fill the hours meaningfully when society says, in effect, 'You aren't needed.' It's hard *not* to feel depressed when each day is like the one before.

It is not just the individual concerned who is affected. The loss of a job may affect the whole family. When you throw the stone of unemployment into the family pond, the ripples wash over everybody: father, mother and children alike. A father − or teenager − at home all day affects the atmosphere in the home. Sometimes, father − or mother − *and* teenager may both be out of work, at home, getting on each other's nerves, no longer part of the community and no longer feeling that they belong.

The theme of the last fifteen years, employment-wise, has been *change*. Oil price increases in 1973 and 1979 resulted in a depressed economy and the most severe output recession of this century. Coupled with this was an information technology revolution which brought technology into every industrial and commercial activity: many jobs which had been done by people were now done by machines.

Heavy industry has declined and there has been a move towards a post-industrial society. There has been a shift from *production* industries (eg, ship-building, steel, engineering and construction) towards service industries (finance, business services, leisure, transport and communications, computer technology). The change has taken place on a nationwide basis. Now, more than three million people are unemployed; factories have closed down; there is devastation in the heart of many of our once-great industrial cities.

If you are unemployed yourself you may hope that the old jobs will come back, that the heavy industries will flourish again and that labour-intensive heavy industry will make a comeback. You will know that this talk of a 'post-industrial' society doesn't give you a job, that a job is, in Freud's words, a person's strongest tie to reality and that your happiness and psychological health depend upon doing *some* kind of work (whether it is paid employment or painting the kitchen).

You may be nostalgic for the past. I visited a northern city and spoke to some youngsters there, working on an urban farm project. They told me they didn't think much of the work. 'What would you like to be doing?' I asked one of the young people. 'A proper job, like my dad used to have − in a factory. Real work,' was the answer.

Work provides people with company (someone to talk to), an opportunity to help others, a chance to feel needed. It provides (to take up Freud's point) links with reality — the community — that prevent us from becoming overwhelmed by fantasy and negative feelings. Work can be beneficial even when it isn't particularly enjoyable: it requires an investment in something outside of the self; the contrast between work and leisure enhances the value of each.

It costs £21 billion per year to pay for unemployment. It is an expensive business. Some politicians, particularly on the Left, would argue that the money could be better spent on a big public works programme, expansion of the caring services and the training of the unemployed (real training for real jobs). Declining industry, they would argue, *could* be revitalized by more investment, by more research and development and by more education and training (especially for the young unemployed). It is calculated that it presently costs £6,800 per annum to keep someone on the dole; it would cost £8,000 per annum to employ them. Some would argue that to find the difference (£1,200 per annum, per individual) is not only politically viable (more tax for those in work, and for the well-off) but morally absolutely necessary.

Unemployment can cause grave psychological harm. It affects both those who have lost their jobs and those who have never worked. More and more of us will be faced, in the years to come, with the problem of what to do with our leisure, as we work shorter hours, retire earlier, work part-time (or are unemployed). This is an age of transition. The industrial age, with all those large shipyards, factories and foundries, may be no more; the age of the micro-chips may be upon us. If it is, it will demand new ideas, new attitudes, new ways of looking at the concept of work. The problem of leisure was solved for many people, in the past, by the Calvinist work ethic. Do we now have to review that ethic?

Work adds purpose to our lives. For some people it supplies a complete purpose: they live for their work. Others work to earn money in order to live. Let's, first, look at the problems of somebody who *has* a job but who finds that being in work doesn't supply her with the meaning that she requires in her life. This is a letter to 'On The Couch' from a young woman for whom work has not provided the answer to loneliness:

148

My life doesn't seem to have any purpose. For the past few years I've been stuck in a boring job with no chance of promotion. Without qualifications I feel there is little else I can do but I can't afford to go back to further education and, anyway, I'm not sure I'd have the perseverance to finish the course if I did.

I still live with my parents and would like to get a flat but I'm scared I'll be without money and won't be able to manage.

I haven't had a relationship with anyone for ages and I feel as though I have become afraid of men. I have my friends but they are dropping away to lead their own lives and I don't like to intrude.

I'd rather like to break away and do something with my life before it is too late. But what? I don't have a talent for anything. I've been pondering for the last two years about what to do with my life. I'm 23 and I don't want to end up alone.

The writer of this letter doesn't appear to have solved any of the three major life-tasks: work, love and friendship. She is bored by her job, has become afraid of men and her friends are rapidly disappearing, going away to lead their own lives. What should she do? Here is part of my answer to her:

Dear B. Let me ask you a question. What is it you want? Until you decide *that* − and have a few clear aims in mind − you will continue to drift. Also, please forget 'Yes, but'. That's a well-worn cop-out. If you say that to each and every suggestion put to you we'll never get anywhere.

You must set yourself *specific goals*. In your domestic life why not aim at being in a flat a year from now? There are other people in a similar situation (or who have already made the break) who would share with you. Find out more about it, use the local paper to make useful contacts, start saving your money. Do it today.

Whilst you're living with your parents you are achieving nothing and perhaps imagine that the world owes you a living and that you are not responsible for your own existence. Both of these ideas are false. Good things will never come to you if you just sit around and wait. Already, you are starting to feel sorry for yourself. Self-pity is useless. It is deeds that count.

Get out from under and *do something* about your situation. Meet other people who − like you − want a place to live and some independence. The money side of it will work out. What you need is a little more confidence in yourself, less fear of the world. The world is neutral. What's in here (our hearts) is just as important as what's out there.

Don't, at this stage, set yourself aims that are too grandiose. Define those areas in which you hope to make progress (domestic, work, friendship, love) and *write down* the goals you hope to reach in each area of fulfilment. Don't say, 'In 1984 I want to emerge as a truly lovely person.' This means nothing and, besides, you said it last year.

Set yourself *sub-goals*. In your work you must aim for (a) a change or (b) promotion. If you choose (b) you must decide what steps to take to impress upon people that you are serious about your job. Sign on for a course in computers, or a foreign language, a higher qualification. Make enquiries about grants, sponsorship. Don't talk vaguely about higher education. Ask two questions. Where do I want to go? (You must decide.) What help is available to get there?

Friendship: you'll make plenty of friends when you learn to live with your own vulnerability. Strength isn't being showy, popular, the life and soul of the party. Real strength lies in recognizing your own weaknesses and allowing others to see them too. I'm sure your friends do not want you to abandon them. Those friends are vulnerable too. Opting out of friendship helps nobody.

Make new friends. There are lots of people who would be glad of your company. Join an organization which does something to help other people; join an evening class, a club of some sort. Doing things together and working for a common goal is the best way I know of making lasting friendships. To make friends, you have to start off by being a little more friendly yourself.

Having decided on your goals (and sub-goals, ie, steps along the way), be determined and committed. Have some fun, too: that's all part of the striving, and the rewards. Don't take yourself too seriously, but take what you're doing very seriously indeed. Get out of your own little world, become involved, committed, to something larger. That will give your life some purpose. Unselfishness is the gateway to love. Remember you. Remember those others.

Forget about failure: there's no such thing. There is only

150

wasted time. Decide now what it is you want and go for it. Don't worry if you fall down once or twice: we all do that. Go fishing, see what you catch. It's better than sitting at home looking at your face in the back of a spoon. In the beginning was the deed and especially that first, brave step.

Get your philosophy right. What's success? It's getting what's right for *you*, not what other people tell you is important. Never imitate others. Choose goals to suit your own personality. In *The Wind in the Willows* Mole needed security, Toad reckless adventure. People have different needs and that's why we must choose goals to suit our own personality. Then we have to start saying 'I can' rather than 'Yes, but'. We're all underachievers; so many of us have too little faith in ourselves.

What you've done with your life so far, B, is build a prison for yourself. The walls consist of your self-doubt: all those 'yes, buts', and 'I can'ts.' Start to say 'I can'. Believe in yourself. You can hardly be more lonely and isolated than you are now.

The cell door is open. Take a look. All you need to do is to walk through that door, one step after the other, to the open sky and the green fields beyond. It will take courage to make the first move but, believe me, it's worth it. Those who get there had to take a first step; after that, they just kept putting one foot in front of the other.

Once out of prison, into the sweet air, you'll see some hills in front of you. Decide which of them *you* want to climb (you can't climb them all) and go up bit by bit. You'll reach the top of the right hill for you if you choose, don't look back and forget about self-pity and failure.

Take your first step today. I wish you a happy journey. It could be very exciting. I wish people had a bit more faith in their own abilities. I know you can make it, B. I believe in you. Now, you have to learn to believe in yourself. You can only do that setting out on the road. Every long march has to start somewhere. I hope you meet somebody you like to share your road with you.

The tone of my reply to B is somewhat breathless, certainly exhortatory. However, there are two aspects of my response to B which I think deserve further elucidation: the notions of (a) self-reliance and (b) fun. Both are important to those who are unemployed as well as employed. Each may suggest a way out of the depression that comes with being in a job which brings no satisfaction or, worse, being without a job at all. Let's look at them in turn:

Self-reliance. It may be the duty of the government to provide jobs for the people but it isn't the duty of the government to teach people how to live. Nobody owes anybody a living. We have to learn to live by asking: 'What would I like to do?' Then, we have to take those steps. Nobody else can do it for us. We have to do it ourselves.

If you are unemployed, you may well feel depressed, bored, anxious, bitter – and angry. Expect those feelings. Then use them, especially that anger. Say: 'This won't do.' Then do something about your situation.

Your first task is *information gathering.* If you are young, go along to your local Careers Officer and find out if there are any jobs or training schemes in your area. If you have had a job – and have good qualifications and experience – get in touch with the Professional and Executive Recruitment. Try to attend one of their job-hunting courses.

Find out whether there are any small firms in your area who need employees. By 1990, small firms are expected to increase their workforce by about 700,000 people, many of them full-time. What are the opportunities for self-employment? Can you get a market stall, buy and sell shoes or second-hand clothes, home-made jewellery, confectionery? Go out and about and see what other people are doing. Offer to help at a stall in the local market. Keep in touch with people who *are* doing something about solving the problem.

Are there any part-time jobs (perhaps in hotels, pubs, restaurants, offices, at the local hospital)? Look in the local paper and see what part-time jobs are available. Check up how part-time employment will affect your benefits. Talking of benefits, make sure that you are getting all you are entitled to. If you're having difficulty, contact the Claimants and Unemployed Workers Union at 120 Standhill Crescent, Barnsley, Yorkshire, S71 1SP.

What is going on in the local community? Whether you live in the city or in the countryside, there will be community activities, YTS programmes, sports clubs and opportunities for voluntary work. Helping people worse off than ourselves, such as the physically or mentally handicapped, is a royal road out of self-pity and may well provide you with the feeling that you are wanted and needed: a viable, human being who has a great deal to offer.

Are there any amateur theatre companies in your area who need volunteers? Can you take up an interest or a hobby (eg, computers, dressmaking, fashion, windsurfing, climbing, the countryside) which may lead on, especially with some further training, to a 'proper job'? If you go to help out at the local theatre, perhaps working back-stage, making props, it *is* keeping you in touch with people who are doing something active and interesting. Their enthusiasm will affect you; it could lead on to further work.

The worst thing to do is to stay in bed all day. Get up. Have a daily programme, including keep-fit activities. Keep fit for what? you ask. For life, for beating the despondency, depression and frustration of unemployment. Get hold of a copy of Guy Danuncey's *The Unemployment Handbook* (National Extension College). It gives practical advice on job hunting and clear explanations of Unemployment Benefit and Supplementary Benefit Rights. Join a club for the jobless. If there isn't one in your area, set one up. It is better to remain positive, active, outgoing: the alternative is hopelessness, despair and loneliness. Human contact is vital: to young people and old people alike. It prevents isolation, self-pity; it keeps your situation in a human perspective.

If you want to do some voluntary work and don't know how to set about it, contact the National Council for Voluntary Organizations, 26 Bedford Square, London WC1 (or enquire at your local Citizens' Advice Bureau). You may be able to assist with Meals on Wheels or help senior citizens with their gardens; you could help in the local hospital or in local playgroups; there may be a group in your area who offer their services, free, to local senior citizens, or to the handicapped. (You can do a number of hours each week and still get unemployment benefit.)

Loneliness is a killer. There has recently been a sharp rise in the rate of teenage suicides. Unemployment, though not the sole cause, is a major factor in this alarming trend. It is, in my view, better to do *anything* rather than sit at home, or lie in bed, doing nothing. Doing nothing is *very* stressful to human beings if it goes on too long. Human contact, belonging to a group, is the antidote to the terrible feelings of meaningless and isolation which afflict the unemployed.

If you are young you may consider working abroad, or working in another part of the country. If you are fed up and 'down', apply to go on an Outward Bound course and try your

153

hand at canoeing, rock climbing, caving, orienteering and underwater swimming. There is a special fund for young people who can't afford the fees. (Contact the Outward Bound Trust, Avon House, 360 Oxford Street, London W1N 9HA, for details.) Go on a cheap bus trip to a seaside town (or hitch-hike). See if there are any jobs there. Go on a holiday with friends (hitch-hike around the country). So long as the DHSS knows where you are so that they can contact you if a job comes up, you are entitled to go off on a holiday and still claim unemployment benefit.

Learn to use your day constructively. Discipline yourself; have a routine. Join a sports club, or a gym, or a social club so that you regularly get out of the house (and meet other people). Keep looking for a job: ask about, know what's going on. Don't resign yourself to never finding a job again. It's estimated that two million (out of the three million currently unemployed) *will* find work. So there is a chance; the situation isn't hopeless; what happens to you – and how you handle that stigma of unemployment – *is* up to you. You can be positive or negative about it. To be negative will be to sink further down a deep well of resentment and despair.

Last year I was going to the post office when a man walked up alongside me. 'Going to sign on?' he asked. I didn't say anything, just walked with him to the DHSS offices and then, making some excuse or other, went on my way. The man, an executive who had been made redundant from a large firm, told me about his former job, his family, his despondency at being out of work. He was an intelligent, sensitive, caring man.

I used to be on the governing body of a school in which 98 per cent of the children – in my day – got jobs. Now, ten years on, very few of those youngsters manage to get a job. They are polite, courteous, children: willing to work, willing to make a contribution to society. To say (as some people still say) that 'the unemployed are idle – they could find jobs if they wanted to' *isn't* true. It's also a terrible slander and injustice.

I have made it clear, I hope, that the government of the day must do all it can to combat unemployment: it must invest in production industry so that we do not have a recurring balance of trade deficit; it must spend more on public works – on sewers, roads, the railways, hospitals, houses, social amenities; it must consistently invest in education and training: of those in schools and colleges, those in jobs and those who are unemployed.

154

Small businesses will be important in the future. There are young unemployed people who *have* been able to convert work experience into a proper job. Through gaining experience in building, car maintenance, dressmaking and fashion, upholstery, catering, computers or marketing they have gone on to set up successful businesses and converted the minus of unemployment into the plus of personal achievement. Governmental concern over unemployment has to be a recurring thread in the fabric of our society. It must be accompanied by self-help. If you don't do it for yourself, who will do it for you?

Perhaps, in the future, there will be more job-sharing, more part-time jobs, earlier retirement, redundancy payments available for those who wish to take them. This will help to give the unemployed, and especially young people, more chance of a job. For a youngster *never* to have worked is a deprivation of human rights. Having said that, I want to turn to the concept of *fun*, and to show that, although work is vital to human beings, it is not the only thing that we are on this planet to do. Life is more than work. Work, like marriage, isn't meant to supply all of our social, emotional and intellectual needs. Work is a large part of life but isn't life itself. Life is for living and that's a much wider activity than work.

Fun. Work, in the industrial past, was for many people a dirty, grinding, back-breaking business. The Calvinist work ethic may have provided a solution to leisure — there was none, or very little — but it certainly did nothing to enhance the *quality* of millions of peoples' lives. My father worked six days a week; on the seventh day he worked in his garden. He didn't have to worry about what to do in his spare time; he simply didn't have any. He also saw little of the world, never went abroad, had one week's holiday a year (day trips to the seaside) and visited London once, after my graduation from university. His life was work, work, work. What kind of a life is that? Is it a full life?

It was for him. He was a contented man. He didn't *know* anything else. How could he *want* anything else? Work, for him, was paid employment. He worked or he and his family starved. He accepted that enjoyment was not a part of work. He worked because he had to. Sometimes he enjoyed his work, sometimes he didn't. That was beside the point. He was, in effect, a wage slave. He *had* to work to get the basic necessities of life.

Most of us are absolved from that relentless grind: that ever-

155

present threat of grinding poverty. Even on Unemployment and Supplementary Benefit we can exist. We exist poorly but we can feed the family, have the basic necessities to exist. We have to cope with a certain amount of poverty. What causes equal distress, in my view, is the *guilt* we feel about not working.

What is work? It isn't merely paid employment. Work is undertaken by millions of people who aren't paid for it. Mothers work, voluntary workers work, so does the amateur thespian, member of the local amateur, rugby or football team, operatic society, keep-fit club. The secretary of the local darts team works, as does the fanatical gardener. If you ask any of these people why they work so hard at what they do, they *don't* say, 'I'm paid for it.' What they say is, 'I enjoy it.'.

The guilt feelings about not working spring from the Calvinist ethic. ('Men must work; women must weep.') We work and in our minds that allows us to take a little time off to enjoy ourselves. Work is something that you do (and are paid for); leisure is something that you enjoy. This definition is clearly not true. I once met a miner on a train. He spent most of the time talking about his racing pigeons. He only mentioned that he was a miner towards the end of the journey. He was besotted with pigeons, and his knowledge on their racing habits was encyclopaedic. I'd say he worked very hard with his pigeons, even though he regarded this as his leisure. Work is *not* always something that somebody pays us to do; it is something we can do in our own time, something that we do because we enjoy doing it.

Play is a child's work and work can be an adult's play. Work and leisure are not so separate, dichotomous, as they sound. The man who erects a greenhouse in his garden is working; he is also doing what he wants to do in his own time. The woman who joins a car maintenance evening class is working; she is also, I hope, enjoying what she is doing. Life is not divided into work and play.

This has enormous implications for the future. Besides those measures already mentioned that have to be taken by the government and by individuals to solve the problem of unemployment, men and women, more and more in the future, *must learn to play*. Leisure will become more available in the future. Many of us will have more time to work out our own leisure activities. None of us should feel guilty about having more leisure time. The work/play we choose to fill the day has

156

just as much validity in terms of human, individual development as paid work. Men and women are at their most human when they play. There is no shame attached to leisure, or unpaid work. You should not feel guilty about enjoying your life.

Play is the way someone learns what nobody else can teach him/her. It is exploration, experiment, adventure, movement. Play is any activity that is indulged in for recreation, interest and amusement. Playing is living. At it lowest it is frivolous; at its highest it is a celebration of being alive. Ovid said in AD 8, that in our play we reveal what kind of people we are. Play is not an optional extra for human beings. It is a vital part of human life, part of being serious about life, part of knowing what life is *for*.

Fun, too, is vital to human beings. Fun comes from doing things together with people you like: it's a by-product, not an aim, and it needn't cost money. You can have fun window shopping with someone you like; some people have fun playing Scrabble; some men I know have fun climbing dangerous mountains. Providing you don't hurt anybody else, have as much fun as you can in your life. It is allowed.

In that marvellous film *One Flew Over the Cuckoo's Nest*, when McMurphy takes the patients out, he doesn't subject them to a lecture, a morally uplifting talk. He takes them fishing, lets them have some fun. He knows that human beings need fun, some of the time, It's a vital element in our mental health.

What we need to do – all of us – in this age of transition, and with the arrival of the post-industrial society, is to get rid of the Calvinist work ethic and to adjust to new notions of what 'work' is. What will count, in future, is a felicitous conjoining of work and leisure (in which paid work will play a less prominent place) and – for the unemployed – a concept of 'good' unemployment in which there will be no stigma attached to not having a paid job.

In 'good' unemployment the individual will still work in a variety of settings, and will be given a wide choice of training schemes (which may, or may not, lead to paid work). He or she will be a respected member of the community, and contribute to that community, doing work which brings him/her dignity, satisfaction and a feeling of belonging. No longer will people ask, 'What do you do?' – and then award a score of 10 if the answer is airline pilot and 0 if the answer is housewife, or labourer. Work will be seen for what it is: something that gives

157

the person — and the community — benefits that accrue from the interests and talents of one unique, individual human being.

You and I have to learn to accept that from now on there will *always* be people unemployed. The number will vary from decade to decade. It will certainly be higher than the number we were accustomed to a decade ago. What we have to do is to redefine employment. (See Peter Warr, *Work, Jobs and Unemployment*, Bulletin of the British Psychological Society, 1983 — Professor Warr is the Director of the MRC Social and Applied Psychology Unit at the University of Sheffield.) We have to try to get rid of 'bad' jobs: jobs which do nothing for the enhancement of the individual and/or impair psychological health. We have to create 'good' jobs: in which people can find satisfaction, personal reward (and have a chance to use their unique talents). Paid work should add to human pride and dignity, not take it away.

We also have to redefine unemployment so that we get rid of 'bad' unemployment, with its stigma and shame and in which individuals have a terrible sense of hopelessness and not belonging. The social reconstruction of unemployment will involve new attitudes towards the place of paid work, unpaid work, leisure and play in all our lives. In terms of work, the future doesn't have to be bleak, if we act with compassion and concern. In terms of personal development, in terms of human creativity and fulfilment, it could be very exciting and rewarding indeed.

Unemployment is a crippling disease. I can only say to everybody who reads this book that unemployment is the concern of all of us. What I hope we will learn from it is lessons that will enhance human dignity and not diminish it. It is up to us. We make or break our world.

If you are a parent of an unemployed youngster, or an unemployed adult, don't give up hope: take a positive attitude towards your situation and do what you can to keep in touch with the community, to work in groups, to build up networks of support so that you avoid the cutting edge of unemployment: loneliness, isolation and loss of meaning in your life. You do have a meaning, and you are entitled to walk on the earth with dignity. Know that and know that what you are is what you do, but that doesn't mean paid work. Know, too, that we are all involved: government, local community, paid workers. You are not alone. The greatest gift that any one of us paid workers can give to somebody who is unemployed is to care.

Chapter 12
Getting yourself together

My sister stayed with us this weekend and we were talking about our childhoods. 'Do you remember,' she asked me, 'the time when mum was drunk, and playing the piano about midnight, and you came into my room and put your arm around me and said, "Don't worry. Everything will be all right"?' I didn't remember but I *can* remember plenty of other times when my mother was drunk and it wasn't a pretty sight.

I don't say this in any sanctimonious, or self-pitying, way. What was, was. I don't think my mother was terribly happy and the bottle was the way out of her depression. It didn't work; that kind of thing doesn't. It gives you a temporary lift, but it solves nothing.

What I told my sister was true, though. As a result of all that chaos in my childhood, I went into psychology to try to find out what was wrong with my mother. I never did. What I learned to do, slowly, was to sort out my own problems and to be less introspective. I also learned that blame and guilt and self-pity were useless. The bottom line is love. All that counts is how much of it you give out to other people.

I learned that if you have suffered yourself, it helps you understand when it happens to other people. It's not pleasant to feel rejected, lost, fragmented. It hurts. Yet, that unbearable pain and dejection *can* give us the impetus to really look at ourselves and sort ourselves out. 'You have to have a chaos within you to give rise to a dancing star,' said Nietzsche. I had the chaos as a child. I'm no rising star, but I do what I can for other people, give what I have to give, do my best, and I'm reasonably happy. Note that I didn't say I was normal. I'm slightly odd but, considering my childhood, I'm incredibly sensible. I've been slightly scarred, but so what? I still have the capacity to love and I firmly believe that it's not what happens to us that counts, but what we make of what happens to us.

159

I've learned that, in order to cope with life, it's the basics we have to get right. Like saying no. It's all right to say no from time to time: you can use that word, with courage and decisiveness, when it's right for you to do so. You want people to love you — you may even be desperate for people to love you because you didn't have enough love in your childhood — but saying yes to everybody *all of the time* doesn't gain other people's love and respect.

I've learned to fix limits on my kindness, so that the love I have to give doesn't turn into resentment. Now, when people phone up and ask me to do something (or ask if they can come to stay here), I ask for details (or ask, 'For how long?'). I don't say yes, and then get angry with them for asking. They have a right to ask. I have a right to fix limits (or say no).

Take a simple example. Your mother-in-law/a friend/a neighbour wants to come over for the afternoon. You say, 'Fine, but I'll have to run you back at 4 pm.' Or say, 'It will be lovely to see you, but you'll have to go at 4 pm. I have a report to write/the children's tea to get ready.' Be definite. State what *you* want. This gives other people a chance to say yes or no (and it saves a great deal of resentment). You may want to be loved, but that doesn't mean you have to be an easy touch, and do what other people want you to do all of the time; that's no way to build up your self-confidence or gain respect and love. You can only do that by sticking up for yourself, saying what you really believe and not being a coward.

Life is tough. The best way to deal with it is to forget the defeats of the past and to know that, in the Here and Now, nothing good will happen to you unless you make it happen. Excuses and yes-buts do nothing to solve the difficulties — or challenges — that come our way. What is needed to deal with life is courage and style. We have to learn to be brave: it takes practice.

Your style is dictated by the inner you. It means doing things in a way that suits you, not being too 'other-directed', playing the game of life — and love — as it suits your unique personality. You can be eccentric, up front, quiet: be what you like as long as you feel comfortable with it. Style doesn't mean having money. It means sticking to who you are and not pretending. As soon as you start to pretend you have let your style slip away.

Forget ideal fictions: the perfect face, figure, man, woman, partner, marriage. Think in terms of percentages and decide for yourself what you will — and won't — settle for. Stick to your decision. If it will do, that's fine. If it won't, say so, then change it. If you don't, who will?

Have a 'me time'. Rewards are vital to human beings. You can't give out to people all of the time without, from time to time, getting some of the things *you* need. No output without input. So insist on some rewards for yourself and don't explain, apologize, feel guilty. You deserve those rewards; they are your right.

Don't leave other people to work out your values for you. Work out your own. School may have stifled your curiosity, branded you as mediocre (or even a failure). Don't accept their label. Work out your own view of yourself and your worth. Value yourself. Re-kindle your sense of enthusiasm, go for something that is worth doing and start to have faith in yourself again.

Have a dream, a purpose. Maybe you would like to see a better world? Join a political party and do something about it. You would like to travel around the world? Start saving up, now, to make the dream come true. Having a purpose does help us to cope with life's crises; it helps us to harness our energies towards a greater goal. 'By their dreams ye shall know them'; tell me your dreams, your hopes, and I'll tell you who you are. Establish space to make something of yourself. Find friends who share the same values. Friends are very important.

Start from today. Write down the things that are important to you, what you have, what you don't have, what you *want*. Work towards them, find people to share your journey, people who will encourage you. Don't be too hard on yourself. Say to yourself, 'I deserve some good things' (because you do). Write down the good things about you and bear them in mind. *You have as much right to be here, on this earth, as anyone else.*

Don't be afraid of change, out there or within you. If your style is no longer working, redefine yourself and find a new style. Shake things up a bit. Talk over your situation with friends you trust and then do something about it. Work towards those changes that are essential to make you grow.

Expect hard times, they happen to all of us, sooner or later. When they come just say, 'This is hard' (or 'This is hell'). It is. What you have to believe is that, if you take it day by day, all that pain, sorrow, suffering, chaos and confusion will pass. The

161

flowers *will* bloom again and you will dance again. From that blackness, that suffering, will emerge a new, stronger you. During those hard times, you must say to yourself, 'This will pass.' When you do emerge, you will know what real emotional pain feels like, and this will enable you to understand and help others who may be suffering. From the suffering and the chaos will come order and a greater humanity, if you let it.

Talk about your pain to others. Other people won't mind; they have been there too. When you've talked about it, and cried, cried, cried, wipe the tears from your eyes and say, 'I'm going to move forward now, and live my life.' Live it with greater joy, wonder and conviction than before. Now you know about pain. You know it can hurt you terribly; but you also know that, with courage, it can be overcome.

Remember, too, never pretend, always be yourself. This doesn't mean you can't take inspiration from people you admire, but you must not adopt somebody else's style, lock, stock and barrel. It may work for them, but it won't work for you. Work out your own opinions and stand by them.

Don't forget to notice the good things in life. Look in awe at the sky at night, wonder at the power of the turbulent sea. The fields, the hedgerows, every garden is full of magic. It seems such a pity to miss the beauty of the earth as we walk around, heads bent in worry, obsessed by material possessions. Your two most precious assets are your health and your sense of wonder. Try to preserve both: don't squander the miracle of being alive on things that don't really matter.

Expose yourself to things that make you feel good. It may be classical music or jazz, the Beatles or gospel music. It may be that you love the theatre, or the ballet, or feel deprived if you haven't seen a good movie for some time. If you need these things − or a walk by the sea − to make you feel alive, make sure you find time for them. We all need inspiration, a lift from time to time, so be selfish and make sure you get something to feed the spirit, as well as the body.

Learn to nurture that inner child within you. Your inner child may moan, complain, grumble now and then. Why not? Just as long as the joyous, brave, optimistic, bold and adventurous inner child within you is also given a chance. Freud said children are 'completely egotistic; they feel their needs intensely and strive ruthlessly to satisfy them'. This may well be true, but they are also spontaneous and magical. They see the world as though

162

everything in it had a fresh coat of paint. They feel life in every limb. They reach out to life. They have adventures, take risks. Adults should do the same. We need the child within. It is a great source of energy, creativeness, happiness — and charm. Here are ten points to remember about being child-like (*note: this is not* the same as being childish):

- *Live in the present.* If you don't start to live now, be less harsh on yourself today, when will you start? Do something child-like today to show that you are beginning to like yourself.
- *Don't try to be an adult all the time.* Join a group which allows you to be a child and express your wonder at this beautiful world. Don't be cynical. Work towards others who want to make this earth better, who have no wish for it to be polluted and destroyed by 'adults'.
- *Find a partner who allows you to have fun, who will allow you to be the child sometimes.* Being a mummy (or daddy) to someone the whole time can be very dispiriting.
- *Get to know your inner child.* Talk to it, be friends with it, tell it when it's not wanted but don't keep it under lock and key for ever. You'll lose the real you if you rush forward to success and leave your child behind.
- *Work through your griefs.* Your inner child may want to grieve, to mourn for a while — over past defeats, lost opportunities, loss of a friend. Cry like a child if you want to and then, through your tears, reach out to the stars and the moon. With rain and sun we can make a rainbow. Our lives don't have to be grey.
- *Don't grow up completely.* I have no wish to read your name in your local paper under 'Deaths'.
- *Never lose your vulnerability.* Just find people with whom you can express it. They too have an inner child. They know we are all a mixture of good and bad and they are much more understanding than you think. Never try to resolve your confusions alone, let others help you.
- *Learn by doing, joining.* Good intentions, fine intentions, don't count. If you join the local operatic society/theatre club/women's group, score 10; if you say you're going to see what's happening locally that might interest you, and you are definitely going to do it tomorrow, score 0.
- *Be good enough.* If you're perfect I, for one, don't wish to

meet you. It's not your eye-shadow, or your 28″ waist that joins us together but your faults and failures − and your sense of fun.

● *Accept yourself*. There is an appalling 4-year-old in you, and one in me. If we know it's there, we can tame it and learn to use that energy of the child for creative, positive purposes. Express your uniqueness fully. This means liking yourself − and those child-like elements within you.

The ability to have fun and be spontaneous are part of a creative attitude to life. They are also important steps in the direction of self-actualization. (See *The Farther Reaches of Human Nature* by Abraham Maslow, Pelican.) Spontaneity implies honesty, truthfulness, naturalness − not imitating other people. It implies an ability to respond to the world without too much striving, and straining, without too much artificiality. To be able to have fun is to be able to celebrate life.

All of us need to let go, to strive a little less hard in the direction of those things that don't matter, and learn to appreciate the things that do. (See *An Experiment in Leisure* by Joanna Field [Marion Milner] Virago.) We all have to learn to find that inner core which is the real being. Life is more than a fridge-freezer and wall-to-wall carpeting. Life is a precious gift. Why not take five minutes of each day to admire one beautiful aspect of the earth or to simply stop striving and just *be*?

Doing nothing isn't wasting time. It's what you do after you've rested − or had a little potter − that counts. Some people never rest, never relax and spend a great deal of energy getting nowhere. You have only got one life, so don't waste it. This means you should take time out to simply relax, enjoy yourself (or do nothing) and look around you. What is the point of making the journey if you don't take a look at what's beautiful in life?

Don't spend you life justifying yourself. You have a right to be wrong from time to time, to make mistakes, change your mind, do things which, on reflection, you wish you hadn't. *Don't* offer elaborate reasons or explanations to justify your behaviour. You were wrong. You made a mistake. The best apology you can make is to get on with your life and be of more use to people. You will be, since you will have learned from your mistake, if you have learned anything at all, that you are not perfect. This makes you of more use to the rest of us.

164

Try to be less anxious. Anxiety is fear spread thin. It feels like fear, but there is no real danger. It gets out of control when upsetting thoughts increase bodily tension (or vice versa) and we have to learn to dispel anxiety by thinking positively, by relaxation, meditation − or resorting to action. When we try to do something that we are scared of, and succeed, then we learn to cope with anxiety (and we learn that most of what we fear is imaginary). To dare is to conquer anxiety. To dare takes courage but what is life if it is to be lived in fear all the time?

Try to be more confident. You have a right to be here. You don't need my permission to breathe, live your life, snatch moments of happiness. If your parents − or somebody else − hasn't given you permission to live, give yourself that permission (or take it from me − I'm not scared of thunderbolts). Women, in particular, need to stand up very tall and say, 'We are part of this earth, slightly over a half of the world's population. We have a right to be on this earth. We have a right to voice our thoughts, to act on our own behalf and to strive for the rights of women.' You can't do this without confidence in yourself.

Such confidence must not rest solely on the good opinions of others, particularly men. It must come from within; from an unshakeable belief that you are worthwhile and that you have something to contribute to the community. If women rely solely on the opinions of the men in their lives, then they remain in danger of never doing anything for themselves, of doing what others want them to do (particularly men). It is not women's job to constantly service men. It is women's job to live creative and fulfilled lives.

Consider the following letter to 'On The Couch' from a young woman who lacks confidence and who is very 'other-directed'. She needs the stamp of approval from others and doesn't realize that, at some stage or other in all our lives, we have to say, 'I'm O.K. I'm not going to seek "so pathetically" for approval from others. I'm going to work out what I believe in and get on with it.' This is the stamp of self-approval and that's the one that counts.

Here is B's letter:

I am in my late teens, still living at home and have had a happy, balanced upbringing. I get on well with my parents, am pretty happy at college and have a good selection of friends. But there's one thing that bothers me.

I've recently realized that my general varying levels of

happiness and doom-and-gloom (which are the same as most people's) depend almost entirely on what I feel my friends (especially my boy-friends) think of me.

I'm sure I could be much happier if only I was self-assured enough not to need approval from others all the time. Perhaps you have an idea of some ways in which I could convince myself that I'm a really worthwhile person, without me relying so pathetically on the approval of other people?

Dear B. Interesting question. At one time I'd have told you that there were only two ways in which we can gain self-confidence: (a) through achievement, setting ourselves goals and reaching them; (b) through the esteem, praise and/or love of people that we respect. That sounds great, but there's something missing.

Put it this way. I once went to Eastwood to visit the house in which D. H. Lawrence was born. In a nearby café, afterwards, I asked an old lady what she thought of D. H. L. ''E were daft, me ducks. 'E follered balloons,' she said. So much for David Herbert.

That old lady was fascinating. She'd weathered some eighty summers and was a bit wrinkled but her personality shone through like a new coin. Her clothes were tatty but she knew exactly who she was and, more important, *she accepted herself*, liked herself. I liked her too. She made me laugh, I felt at ease in her company, I didn't need to pretend.

How many of us really like ourselves? I know quite a few lovely people who are riddled with self-doubt. One of them was told by her man recently, 'I love you.' She asked me, 'Does he, really?' That's silly. She doesn't have to run away with him (or do anything else for that matter), but she should take it as a compliment: not as proof of the man's poor taste or total lunacy.

The first thing we have to do is to say, loud and clear, 'I'm me.' We have to learn to like ourselves and to live with ourselves. Why not believe it if somebody says, 'You're beautiful'? In their eyes you are. They may have the right attitude, not you.

This *liking yourself* factor is even more vital than achievements or the positive comments of friends. It would explain why that lady over there (the one with a figure like a punctured water-bed) enjoys life, has lots of friends and is very relaxed: whilst you and I are scanning the mirror worried sick about our spots.

166

Women are particularly prone to self-doubt, and I'm not surprised. They have to contend with men (not easy) and with their own natures. Give a man a train set and he's happy; women are slightly more complicated, they want men who are dependable *and* exciting, mysterious *and* rugged, moody, broody *and* fun to be with. Women want life to be safe and predictable *and* to be dangerous, surprising. It's a lot to ask.

Disappointment lowers the self-esteem of many women. I'm sure D. H. Lawrence wondered whether he was a bit crazy. He wanted us to *live*, to be alive to passion and love, to open our eyes to the beauty of the universe and for us not to be strangers to each other or exiles in a world to which we all belong. 'If I had a man like Alan Bates in *Women in Love* I'd surprise everybody,' a lady told me last Christmas. They're hard to come by. Women must be as crestfallen as Lawrence when they look around them at the real world. It could be a lot better, especially concerning love.

Men can't all be Birkins explaining about figs but they needn't all be Arthurs, going on about darts. It must be difficult for women to gain self-respect when – a great deal of the time – they get the wrong signals for men. 'What's for tea?' is a question that's unlikely to make a woman reach for the smelling salts or go weak at the knees.

Women do very odd things to cope with the conflict (reality vs romance) within them. What they do is the stuff of great novels, searching, at terrible inconvenience, for somebody (usually a man) who will only see them as they would like to be seen, treat them as they desire to be treated.

With men you have to be brave and speak out: tell them relationships aren't about sexual prowess and sex objects. They are about sensitivity and building each other up, not belittling them. Women have enough trouble as it is balancing their need for domesticity and stability with their longing for love. To have to cope with brutish/boring males as well is enough to make any woman wonder whether she is in her right mind. She is: her values are right. The values of the world are wrong. They were given to us by men.

Women really must become stronger, lean on each other more, help each other out, if they are to be rid of the victim complex; their futile dependence on other people, waiting for the compliment that's never going to come (not from him). They must learn to accept the opposing sides of their own

167

personalities and to follow their ideals in which direction they can, helping each other. Then, they'll gain self-respect, self-assurance, a solid self-regarding sentiment which isn't at the mercy of any man who comes along who whispers those three potent words: 'I love you.'

That's it, then, B. Achieve your goals. Try hard. Accept the regard of others but − vital, this − don't totally lean on that. Learn to accept yourself, with all your faults, all your inner conflicts, yearnings, disappointments. Learn to live with the feelings within you. The fact that you aren't perfect makes you like the rest of us.

If your boyfriends compliment/love/adore you, accept that. It's their decision. Don't fall about trying to please them: just follow your own star. If they're going your way, go together. If they're not, sort it out (say something) or wish them adieu. This can be a world of love if we hold on to that idea, never let go of it. Start off by liking yourself. You is all you have. You've got to believe it.

I went to the park last night. I cast a few breadcrumbs on the waters for our feathered friends. 'You're daft, me ducks,' I shouted to them. A man near by gave me a funny look. What the hell do I care? I'll do it my way. I have a right to be here. We all have − men *and* women.

Life isn't just about coping. Life is about living. Coping is managing, getting by, having no choice but to struggle on as best you can. There will be times in your life when you will be coping (and glad to cope). There will be times in your life − I hope − when you're ready to move forward to living.

What is living? Living is fulfilling your needs. At one time I used to give a set-piece lecture called 'The Needs of Children'. Those needs included love, stimulation, new experiences, praise, prestige, responsibility. It dawned on me after some time (psychologists can be incredibly dim-witted) that the needs of children were, to a fairly large extent − also the needs of adults. Children need friends, someone to talk to, little adventures, activities which will boost their confidence. They need fun, enjoyment, movement, laughter, companionship. So do adults.

I can tell you your needs. I can tell you mine and tell you what made me move from coping to living, what made me make choices rather than to accept life as it was dished out to me. The things that helped me make that huge leap in the direction of life were:

168

1   *A sense of Good.* Some people call this God. It doesn't
    matter, so long as you can look at a flower and marvel,
    see the beauty in the earth and wonder. There are bad
    people but there are very good people too. I've made my
    choice. I believe in the good, and in the triumph of good;
    that's a positive choice. The alternative road leads you to
    cynicism and/or despair.
2   *The past is dead.* You remember it. It can, with its ghosts,
    those memories, still hurt you. Remembering the hurt of
    the past solves nothing. The only thing that counts is to
    give all the love you have to give in the Here and Now.
3   *A sense of self.* A sense that I am absolutely unique, a
    one-off, a book about life with a print run of one. (So are
    you.) I have no sense of arrogance as I say this. It is a
    fact. It is up to me to work out how the story ends. I work
    out the plot of my own life and should expect nobody else
    to do it for me.
4   *Community feeling.* A sense of self isn't selfishness.
    Selfishness, to live for yourself, is the road to nowhere.
    It is by working for and alongside others that we achieve
    our potential and create a world fit for ourselves and
    others to live in. The Me generation is past; the We
    generation is here to stay.
5   *Realistic expectations.* Pain and suffering will come my
    way. It will not alter my perception of the world. I know
    that the world is a tough place. I will not seek to blame
    others for my misfortunes but will strive as bravely as I
    can to overcome them. Courage is vital.
6   *Little adventures are crucial to living.* I take time out to
    have little adventures. They're important to my sanity,
    my spontaneity and to my belief in myself that I can meet
    challenges, new experiences, and come away refreshed
    and enhanced by them. There's no security in life. The
    only certainties in life are death and taxes. Any security
    we have comes from within us. From time to time that
    security, that sense of competence and inner worth,
    should be put to the test.
7   *Friends are vital.* I need someone to signal: 'You're OK.'
    This enables me to give that signal to other people. It is
    an important signalling system. It is mutual affirmation
    and none of us can live without it.
8   *I'm me.* I am not my mother. You are not my mother. I

169

won't blame you for what she lacked, what she did. I won't blame her. It wasn't my fault (or yours). There'll be no identity confusion. I'm me and I'll do you the favour of allowing you to be you.

9   *I'm not normal.* I'm much better than that. I'm just a little bit crazy. Sometimes, in the evening, I walk down to the sea and shout, 'Joy, love, adventure, creativity, fun, friendship, courage.' I believe in them all. That's why I shout the words out, very loud. They're important. (If you don't live by the sea shout them in the garden/lavatory – just so long as you believe in what you're saying.)

10   *Help others.* Don't spend a life-time licking your psychological wounds, picking at the scabs of those defeats – or that terrible pain – from the past. What good is that? There are some marvellous people out there. Join them, give out what you have to give. Life is about giving. All that is left, when life is over, is the love you gave to others.

I love my sister. She is a very beautiful person. After her visit, she phoned me up. 'I felt very funny talking about us when we were kids,' she told me. 'You must never be frightened of the past,' I told her. 'The things that you thought might destroy you then, didn't. You survived, and you'll survive equally frightening things in future.' That fear is the fear of a little child. When you were a child, you were afraid as a child; that's why the fear was so intense. Now, as an adult, you must be brave. Those things won't harm you because you have learned to look the wild things straight in the eye and ignore their horrible teeth and be brave.

It takes mess to make a car, paint a painting, create a worthwhile life. But we'll dance, you and I. We'll learn not just to cope but to live and Good will wipe away the tears from our eyes and we'll give out to others, in joy and wonder, at the miracle of human life. From the chaos will come order and from the evil will come good – that's what I believe. I hope you believe it too. What would life be if we believed otherwise? We would merely repeat the mistakes of the past. I truly believe that isn't necessary, not if you have courage – and love. Love for one's fellow beings is the bottom line.

170

Useful addresses

Note: for legal and financial advice, together with information regarding a wide variety of problems, you should consult your local Citizens' Advice Bureaux – their numbers can be found in your local directory. For information regarding the self-help groups and supportive organizations, you should enquire at the local reference library.

Pregnancy   British Pregnancy Advisory Service, Guildhall Buildings, Navigation Street, Birmingham 2. 021–643–1461. *Or* 7 Belgrave Road, London SW1. 01–222–0985.
  Family Planning Association, 27–35 Mortimer Street, London W1N 7RJ. 01–636–7866.
Birth   National Childbirth Trust, 9 Queensborough Terrace, London W2 3TB. 01–229–9319.
Mothers and Children   National Childminding Association, 204–6 High Street, Bromley, Kent, BR1 1PP. 01–464–6164.
  Pre-School Playgroups Association, 61–3 Kings Cross Road, London WC1X 9LL. 01–833–0991.
Fathers and Children   Families Need Fathers, 97c Shakespeare Walk, London N16 8TB. 01–254–6680.
Parent Support   Organization for Parents Under Stress (OPUS), 106 Godstone Road, Whyteleafe, Surrey, CR3 0EB. 01–645–0469.
Lone Parents   National Council for One Parent Families, 255 Kentish Town Road, London NW5 2LX. 01–267–1361.
  Gingerbread, 35 Wellington Street, London WC2E 7BN. 01–240–0953.
  Child Poverty Action Group, 1 Macklin Street, Drury Lane, London WC2B 5NH. 01–242–9149 and 3225.
Family   National Marriage Guidance Council, Herbert Gray College, Little Church Street, Rugby, Warwickshire, CV21 3AP. 0788–73241.
Education   Advisory Centre for Education (ACE), 18 Victoria Park Square, London E2 0PB. 01–980–4596.
Health   Health Education Council, 78 New Oxford Street, London WC1A 1AH. 01–631–0930.
Leisure   Sports Council (England), 16 Upper Woburn Place, London WC1H 0QP. 01–778–8600.
  Scottish Sports Council, 1 St. Colme Street, Edinburgh EH3 6AA. 031–225–8411.

Sex Problems Brook Advisory Centre, 233 Tottenham Court Road, London W1. 01–580–2991 and 01–323–1522. (Advice on contraception, pregnancy, abortion).
National Marriage Guidance Council (address as above. Advice to couples aged 16 or over, married or not).
Divorce National Council for Divorced and Separated, 62 Stourview Close, Mistley, Manningtree, Essex. 020–639–6206.
Mental Health Mind (National Association for Mental Health), 22 Harley Street, London W1. 01–637–0741.
Drugs Release, 169 Commercial Road, London E1 6BW. 01–837–5602.
Drugs Advisory service (look up telephone number in local directory).
Despair & Suicide The Samaritans (look up telephone number in local directory. The Samaritans will help in any crisis but especially if somebody is depressed and considering suicide.)
Legal & Financial National Council for Civil Liberties, 21 Tabard Street, London SE1 4LA. 01–403–3888.
Citizens' Rights Office, 5 Bath Street, London EC1V 9QA. 01–405–5942. (Advice and help on social security problems.)
Citizens' Advice Bureaux (National Association), 115–23 Pentonville Road, London N1 9LZ. 01–833–2181. (Look in phone book for local Citizens' Advice Bureaux.)
Homosexuality London Gay Switchboard 01–837–7324. (For teenagers who are gay − or are not sure about it − and wish to talk to someone.)
Bereavement Cruse, Cruse House, 126 Sheen Road, Richmond, Surrey TW8 1VR. 01–940 4818.